KU-186-437

# THE MANAGEMENT OF SPECIAL NEEDS IN ORDINARY SCHOOLS

# EDUCATIONAL MANAGEMENT SERIES
Edited by Cyril Poster

Staff Development in the Secondary School
*Chris Day and Roger Moore*

Challenges in Educational Management
*W.F.Dennison and Ken Shenton*

Preparing School Leaders for
Educational Improvement
*K.A. Leithwood, W. Rutherford and R. Van der Vegt*

Support for School Management
*A.J. Bailey*

Restructuring Universities: Politics and Power in the
Management of Change
*Geoffrey Walford*

Education and the US Government
*Donald K. Sharpes*

Managing the Primary School
*Joan Dean*

Evaluating Educational Innovation
*Shirley Hord*

Teaching and Managing: Inseparable Activities in Schools
*Cyril Wilkinson and Ernie Cave*

Schools, Parents and Governors: A New Approach to Accountability
*Joan Sallis*

Partnership in Education Management
*Edited by Cyril Poster and Christopher Day*

Management Skills in Primary Schools
*Les Bell*

Special Needs in the Secondary School: The Whole
School Approach
*Joan Dean*

# The Management of Special Needs in Ordinary Schools

EDITED BY
NEVILLE JONES AND TIM SOUTHGATE

ROUTLEDGE
London and New York

First published 1989
by Routledge
11 New Fetter Lane, London EC4P 4EE
29 West 35th Street, New York, NY 10001



Printed and bound in Great Britain by
Biddles Ltd, Guildford and King's Lynn



*British Library Cataloguing in Publication Data*

The management of special needs in ordinary
schools. — (Educational management series).
1. England. Schools. Special education.
Planning.
I. Jones, Neville II. Southgate, Tim
III. Series
371.9′0942

ISBN 0-415-00585-X

*Library of Congress Cataloging in Publication Data*

The Management of special needs in ordinary schools.
p. cm.
Includes index.
ISBN 0-415-00585-X
1. Special education. 2. Mainstreaming in education. I. Jones,
Neville, 1930– . II. Southgate, Tim, 1946–
LC3965.M274 1989
371.9–dc19 88-32181
CIP

## CONTENTS

## LIST OF CONTRIBUTORS

**Howard Brayton:** Adviser for Special Educational Needs in Oxfordshire, with responsibilities for pupils aged 14 to 19.

**Tim Brighouse:** Professor of Education, Keele University.

**Nigel Collins:** General Adviser for 14 to 18 education in East Sussex. Formerly adviser for vocational education in Oxfordshire and TRIST Co-ordinator.

**Mike Deans:** Adviser for Special Educational Needs in Oxfordshire with responsibilities for able pupils.

**Cliff Denton:** Research Officer, Oxford University Department of Educational Studies.

**Rhys Evans:** Teacher on the staff of Groby Community College, Leicester.

**Pru Fuller:** Director of the ACE Centre, Oxford.

**David Galloway:** Lecturer in Education, School of Education, Lancaster University.

**John Hanson:** Senior Adviser for Curriculum Studies, Oxfordshire.

**Frank Hodgson:** Tutor in Special Education, Leeds Polytechnic.

**Neville Jones:** Principal Educational Psychologist, Oxfordshire, and Director of LEA Disaffected Pupil Programme.

**Patrick Leeson:** Adviser for Communication and Language Development, Croydon. Formerly evaluator for the Oxfordshire LAP programme.

**Keith Postlethwaite:** Lecturer in Education, Reading University.

**Caroline Roaf:** Special Needs Support Teacher, Peers School, Oxford

**Jackie Sunderland:** Research Assistant at the Oxford University Department of Educational Studies.

**Tim Southgate:** Headteacher, Ormerod School, Oxford, where the National Aids to Communication Centre (ACE) is based.

**Alan Trotter:** Course Director and Principal Lecturer for in-service B.Ed., Leeds Polytechnic.

## FOREWORD

Although the literature on special educational needs has much proliferated in recent years, I know of no book that has approached the topic as comprehensively as this. Contributors and editors alike rightly reject narrow definitions of special needs and, in many ways, this book is a plea for more effective teaching and learning strategies for all. Patrick Leeson, writing of the Lower Attaining Pupils Programme, and John Hanson, writing of the Oxfordshire Skills Programme, severally indicate the progress that derives from Feuerstein's concept of Instrumental Enrichment. Nigel Collins and Jackie Sutherland similarly offer cogent criticisms of the way in which the curriculum content and methodology of some schools actually create pupils whose response to their lack of ownership of their learning processes leads to their designation as disturbed and maladjusted.

The importance of appropriate in-service training in management, using methodologies, incidentally, that are highly analogous to those advocated for effective student learning in other chapters of the book, is emphasised by Frank Hodgson and Alan Trotter.

Both editors make substantial contributions. Neville Jones writes with authority on Welfare and Needs in Secondary Schools; and Tim Southgate writes movingly on both the integration in mainstream of special educational needs students and, with Pru Fuller, on the outstanding work for the physically and mentally impaired of the Aids to Communication in Education Centre in his Oxfordshire school.

Appropriately, since much of the credit for the broad - one is tempted to say all-embracing - sweep of educational innovation in Oxfordshire, the opening chapter is the work of the Chief Education Officer, Tim Brighouse. In it, he demonstrates convincingly that managerial skills are what make effective schools; and that effective schools are the product of LEAs with concern for the individual and vision. He observes with customary forthrightness that present government educational policies are divisive and are undermining the relationships between LEA and school that have led to the high renown, locally and further afield, of education in Oxfordshire.

Cyril Poster

# INTRODUCTION

The main purpose of this book is to point a direction for the management of schools as this relates specifically to special educational needs. Its overall theme is that of good management and effective teaching in secondary education but the issues raised have equal validity for management in other parts of the education system, not least in primary and further education. The specific aim of the book is to explore ways in which school management, through normal curriculum and teaching methods, can be developed to secure an appropriate educational response to the needs of all pupils in a school. This is in contrast with much of present-day planning for pupil needs where for one group of pupils, those with special educational needs, the management task is pursued as a separate and distinct activity.

Everard (1984) has described management in the following way. A manager is someone who:

- knows what he or she wants to happen and causes it to happen;
- is responsible for controlling resources and ensuring they are put to good use;
- promotes effectiveness in work done, and the research for continual improvement;
- is accountable for the performance of the unit he or she is managing, of which he or she is part;
- sets a climate or tone conducive to enabling people to give of their best.

Effective school management is about the management of people, managing the organisation and managing change. All this, together with those aspects of management outlined by Everard, is what is required if schools are to be organised in terms of whole school planning.

The normal school has been defined as the place from which many of those who are difficult to teach have been removed. Special needs are now, however, part of normal school activities. But headteachers have few, if any, guidelines to help them with school management where a significant number of pupils with special needs remain in the school.

## Introduction

Two management systems organised under one managerial roof are possible, and indeed common in industry, but make little sense in education. This is particularly true if the two systems compete for scarce resources, if there is not a utilisation of teacher skills of all kinds to meet pupil needs throughout a school and if competition is set up between subject teachers and those engaged primarily with work in the school's welfare network (Jones, 1988). Dualism has always bedevilled educational systems, and this is even more true now that the management of special needs has become a concern of headteachers in ordinary schools and not just of those in segregated provision.

The problem that arises from having two structures of management, one for special and one for other needs, has a parallel in schools where pupils needs are demarcated as between the academic and the personal, as with some systems of pastoral care. One outcome of this kind of planning and organisation is that two standards of teaching, expectations of pupil learning and staff professionalism are created. Nowhere does this find more explicit expression than in the way we regard some pupils as normal - and not subject to statementing under the 1981 Education Act - and others as less than normal - statemented pupils - simply because they have certain educational needs not shared by other pupils. Such procedures create all kinds of divisions for pupils, for teachers and for parents even within an institution which regards itself as having a coherent policy.

Furthermore, systems of management that divide pupils in this way bring into being separate contexts and climates for learning. Special contexts are frequently devalued if only because there seems to be an inherent tendency in human affairs to stigmatise any minority group which has been identified as receiving, through some form of positive discrimination, some extra help. It is difficult to understand how any school can create for itself a sense of wholeness, with which all who belong can identify, when separate management systems dictate pupil experiences which are at variance with whole school policies, even when these policies ostensibly favour integration. If there is one claim on the education service that those with special educational needs can make it is to have access to the best teaching that schools can offer.

In schools where pupils are divided into normal sheep and special goats then curriculum entitlement is seldom an option.

The issue of management of special needs in ordinary contexts has received little attention at the level of initial teacher training. On in-service courses for teachers the emphasis has usually been towards informing teachers about the problems of educating in special environments pupils with needs. Substantial parts of these courses are geared to organising trips to special schools and lectures are given by those who are expert in the education provided in special environments. On the one-term mangement courses for headteachers the special needs option has had very low priority (Sayer, 1987); and special educational needs scarcely featured as a concern in the 20-day courses, until a number of pilot courses were introduced (Salmon and Poster, 1988). A consequence of all this is that headteachers are only aware of the management system that has been worked out and applied to special schools and units away from ordinary schools. It is not surprising, therefore, that management for special needs in ordinary schools has meant the importation of managerial styles which, while possibly appropriate in special school environments, have little applicability to ordinary schools. As a result we often have what is a rather bizarre system of mangement in ordinary schools where pupils, their teachers and equipment exist independently of other resources and organisation, but cling, limpet-fashion, to an existing school organisation which is geared to not having pupils with special educational needs on the campus. This is not true of all ordinary schools and already, through such mechanisms as the modular curriculum, new styles of school management are emerging. These have the characteristics both of good mangement and of teaching which is appropriate and effective.

This book has been compiled to provide some discussion on the issues; to give illustrations about the kind of curriculum planning and content that is relevant; to encourage those who are working slowly towards whole school practices in situations where the traditional response to the certain needs of pupils has been that of partition.

Contributors to the book were invited to describe their work, to illustrate some of the principles related to a coherent style of school management and teaching and to place emphasis on how to avoid some of the difficulties which arise from separating special management from management of a school as a whole. To this extent, this book has no pretensions to being a theoretical treatise on management and special needs. Neither does it attempt to offer detailed chapter and verse on how school management and specialised work for some individual pupils and their needs should be formulated or projected. This issue of management coherence in ordinary schools, with its relevance to meeting special needs, is an area which has been extensively investigated by one of the editors, Tim Southgate, through the experience of integrating physically disabled pupils from a special school into primary, middle and comprehensive schools in Oxfordshire. It is also of central interest to the other editor, Neville Jones, working from the perspective of educational psychology and currently through the Oxfordshire Disaffected Pupil Programme. The Programme is one of enquiry, research and innovation, linking together individuals and professional groups for the purpose of enhancing pupil learning experiences and opportunities; this to be achieved through the energies of a wide network of professionals engaged in enlarging and strengthening the corporate management of schools and teaching. This is likely to be a shared activity of all those who are engaged full-time in the work of schools or are part of support services to schools, for the mutual benefit of all pupils that attend ordinary schools, whatever their individual needs.

## REFERENCES

Everard, K.B. (1984) Management in Comprehensive Schools, University of York, Centre for the Study of Comprehensive Schools.

Jones, N.J. (1988) 'Welfare and pupil needs', in Jones, N. and Sayer, J. Management and the Psychology of Schooling, Basingstoke, Falmer Press.

Salmon, J. and Poster, C.D. (1988) 'The management of special educational needs', in Poster, C.D. and Day, C. (eds), Partnership in Educational Management, London, Routledge.

Sayer, J. (1987) Secondary Schools for All? Strategies for Special Needs, London, Cassell.

# PART 1: MANAGEMENT AND SCHOOLS

# 1 EFFECTIVE SCHOOLS AND PUPIL NEEDS

Tim Brighouse

## INTRODUCTION

The first part of this chapter attempts to provide an impression of an effective school and suggests a classification of schools. I want to go on to describe what I think are the processes through which schools become effective. We can then look at the evidence which schools themselves use to judge their effectiveness. Finally, I want to examine some of the implications of the government's proposals to legislate for a national curriculum, the retrenchment that will take place if teachers are required to engage in assessing pupil learning at ages 7, 11 and 14, and the way this will have a considerable effect on the majority of pupils who are not engaged in learning directed towards formalised state examinations which in reality is a provision for the select few. Included amongst this number is a significant proportion of pupils with special educational needs.

It is ironic that, apart from the HMI document 'Ten Good Schools' (1977) there is practically no consideration of the effective school in all the many HMI and DES documents of the last ten years. Even the White Paper 'Better Schools', which might have been expected to give attention to the issue, failed to do so. There are, of course, other studies from different agencies and such research findings as found in Rutter _et al._'s (1979) publication.

This omission is explained in part by the diversity of opinion about what is a good or effective school and, therefore, the elusiveness of the topic. In some strange way the sum of the parts of the effective school is exceeded by the totality of what it stands for.

Nor is this a topic which can be tackled by an examination of the obverse side of the coin: it is easy to identify the really ineffective school. Perhaps that is why the media concentrate on bad schools in the hope that by identifying their qualities other schools would know what to avoid. Merely to avoid evil, however, does not guarantee virtue; indeed it might be argued that a preoccupation with adequacy, incompetence and downright inefficiency involves such close scutiny of its qualities that one is, as it were, adversely affected by the experience. One thing that is certain, however, is that schools which look over their shoulders too often, schools which seek to interpret the latest whim of society, are uncertain schools. They are schools that do not know for what they stand. Such schools - just like complacent schools - will never be good or effective schools. Just as the good citizen is not simply one who avoids crime, so the good school is not merely to be defined by being safely indistinguishable from the next. Nevertheless to establish effective schools and colleges constitutes the major part of a local authority's business. If it could get that right, the LEA would have reasonable claim to being itself effective in the major part of its business.

## THE EFFECTIVE SCHOOL

Some of the best literature on the topic is illuminating and positive, descriptive, and relies little on quantified evidence and research, preferring instead a subjective impressionistic view of quality. It is none the worse for that.

An effective school can first and foremost be recognised through its pupils, its staff and its community. Recognition is not solely from the office, from the headteacher or the newspaper; nor will it be necessarily through brochures or speech days - important though they may be - that you know of the effective school. It will be rather from parents who say 'My child simply cannot wait to go to school ... We are doing this survey with Jane because she has brought it home from school and is so insistent that we take part in its completion'. It will be from the kitchen staff or the cleaners who comment, 'It's alright up at Bluebells. Their head is a real good sport. I go there for the people and not the money and I wouldn't miss it for the world.' Or it will be from the community represented perhaps by the local employer's comment, 'We'd always take one from St. Thomas. They always seem to produce such willing and confident youngsters.' Such are the comments that will be heard about the effective school in its local community.

Litmus tests of outstanding schools, therefore, are not just public occasions or examination results but also and importantly private witnesses. Of all connected with the school, the non-teaching staff can tell the depth of the quality of the relationships in the school and can readily see readily whether the school truly celebrates all its constituents. They see beyond the honours board to the consistency of treatment of one another. Ultimately the effective school is discerned in the confidence of its pupils and their commitment to future personal development. They are not merely happy, they are unafraid, free, self-disciplined and autonomous. So often the ordinary school celebrates the few and misleads or even disables the many.

**Shared values**

The outstanding and effective school will have a set of articles - not of course the Articles of Government which every school must have - but almost articles of faith, a kind of collective creed. The jargon phrase often used to describe this phenomenon is a 'shared value system'. The school as a whole, especially the teaching and non-teaching staff, will have a high level of agreement on the purpose of the school.

I do not mean unexceptionable and vague generalisations which adorn education text books but the certainty of a shared value system. Such schools know where they stand on race, the equality of the sexes, on the place of the family in society, matters of prejudice and educational philosophy, because they have discussed these issues sometimes to the point of exhaustion. From this certainty the important everyday rules and habits of the community flow. The certainty informs the marking system, the personal records, arrangements for games, time given to music and residential trips - in short, every activity of the school community.

## Self evaluation

One of the means of achieving such a shared value system is the sensitive use of the processes of self evaluation - eschewing perhaps initially the accountability end of the spectrum with associated implications of self-justification or defensiveness - in favour of an emphasis on common school purposes which depend on interdependence and collegiality.

Such shared value systems are more difficult to achieve in a society which has become more pluralist and tolerant of diversity and where perhaps the pervasive and powerful influences of institutions such as the church and the extended family can no longer be assumed. Moreover, the purpose of schooling has simultaneously become more ambitious. In former times it was more straightforward to achieve a shared value system in primary schools which would be judged by their success rate at eleven-plus or in the grammar school, with the view of ability which was narrowly intellectual - even if monocularly ungenerous - and based on flawed research for its justification. The shared value systems achieved may have been flawed - they may, for example, have undervalued the wider range of human ability and have depended for their existence on the failure of the majority, many of whom had talents which were never uncovered and for whom schooling was an experience to be got out of the way as soon as possible - but they were at least clear and realisable.

## A set of principles

It is more difficult to espouse the value systems of the comprehensive, primary and secondary schools especially when most of the organisational features are inherited from the previous selective system. The teachers of one school, during a reconsideration of their self-evaluation, expressed their value system - which is, of course, distinct from their aims and objectives - broadly if idealistically as follows:

- children should be treated as they might become rather than as they are;
- all pupils should be equally valued;
- teachers should have the expectation that all their students have it in them to walk a step or two with

genius, if only they could identify the talent to find the key to unlock it;
- the staff unitedly should stand for the successful education of the whole person;
- the staff should contribute to the development of mature adults for whom education is a lifelong process and proposed to judge their success by their students' subsequent love of education;
- the staff should try to heal rather than to increase diversities, to encourage a self-discipline, a lively activity to breed lively minds and good health, a sense of interdependence and community.

The effective school will test all its practices - its systems of marking, recording, appointments, publications, its staff development systems, its curriculum, its communications system, structure and system of community relationships - against these principles. It will necessarily find mismatch but will ceaselessly attempt to bring its practices closer to its principles.

## Leadership

In this task the school will depend on successful leadership. In the DES document 'Ten Good Schools', and all other literature, there is the underlying importance of the presence of an outstanding headteacher. The importance of leadership was brought home when a colleague commented on the paradox in one primary school where all the teachers were good, even outstanding, and yet the school could not be called effective. What had happened was the departure of an outstanding headteacher who had been replaced by a very ordinary, even inadequate, newcomer. Slowly the edge was disappearing from the school. Conversely we agreed there was another school which was outstanding although a few years ago we would have thought it ordinary, even humdrum. The collective growth in the school's imperatives seemed to have spurred on all staff to the point where ordinary teachers were performing above themselves, the children had new-found confidence and assurance. Of course, a new and skilful headteacher had arrived.

Our leadership in schools may be divided into three categories. The first category displays a style which leads researchers into classroom practice to call its practitioners 'perceptive professional developers'. Such headteachers would see their role above all as requiring experience and insight based on a deep understanding of their own position on educational and social issues; they would, however, eschew imposing views on others. They regard their role as enjoyable and enriching to themselves as they develop their own skills as well as those of others. They are sharp at identifying the necessity for change and have a deep understanding of its nature. Galton (1980), in the 'ORACLE' survey, gave high marks for success to classroom teachers who were 'infrequent changers'. Every now and then such teachers changed their arrangements, changed their style, the style of the classroom organisation, and improved the quality of children learning. So it is for the first category of school leadership.

The 'perceptive professional developers' give attention to and have an active interest in the curriculum where the change needs to be most frequent. It needs to be most frequent because the teacher must meet individual needs and catch the interests of a multitude of different young people. New materials, new courses, a new environment (in the sense of being new to the teacher or the department concerned) are justified by the expansion of information and the consequential need to replace the old and irrelevant with the new and relevant.

New skills are also cherished but the older ones are cast off only after a deliberate reflection of outworn usefulness. In the curriculum, therefore, the 'perceptive professional developer' knows that information needs to change more frequently than skills and that attitudes need to be fairly consistent in the school as a derivative of their shared value systems. Such leaders see themselves as conductors or perhaps the first violin and the staff basically as colleagues in an orchestra. They may be flamboyant or you may not notice them - styles are legitimately different after all. Such headteachers recognise teachers' different strengths and work so as not to produce a false model to those teachers. Such leaders have the breadth of vision in their appointments to bring to their orchestra new instruments and new performers. They are often good at improvisation: they look for harmony rather than discord to see the necessity for hard argument and debate.

Such leaders have a keen interest in others and see themselves as facilitating the development of those people. Such headteachers will not be absent too long from the school. Such a category of school will change the organisational structure less frequently - perhaps only to give new perspective for teachers and other staff and the learners themselves in order to maximise the opportunity of shared perceptions. So the timetable, pastoral systems of posts and responsibilities, and the departmental arrangements are changed, but only with enormous care since they provide the everyday bearings of support and stability on which the community depends.

The 'perceptive professional developers' see the importance of the bits and pieces: the note of thanks, the particular potential and failing of each member of the community and his or her different need of support, the chronic and acute personal problems of his or her senior colleagues, none in themselves important in the grand scheme of things but everyone, however, vital for the performance of the school as a whole. Such leadership is of course a plural quality. It is exercised at all levels, heads of department and co-ordinators, for example, and for all the people there are in the school.

The second category of leadership produces people who can best be called 'the system maintainers'. They are characterised by their wish 'to keep things on an even keel' and to preserve the existing order of things in order to maintain high standards. They fear precedents which might weaken previous success and are alarmed by change which might precipitate declining standards. They eschew virtually all change. They do not take risks. They like order in all that they do. In establishments run by 'system maintainers' you will find comments like these:

- We tried that in so-and-so's time and it didn't work.
- Why do you want to upset everything that has worked for so long?
- Yes, that is a good idea: if only we could consider it but I fear we cannot because...
- That would set a precedent which would have alarming implications.

Such schools have some way to go to be really effective. They will achieve success of a sort but they will never have that sharp observation which will find the talent of every child. You can tell when they are getting near to moving towards success. It is when they try something different and confess to the thrill of unexpected enjoyment. You can also tell when they are en route towards the third category. It is when you hear more frequently the comment 'Things are not what they used to be' or 'Many leaders are instinctively system maintainers'. They are too distrustful of change.

The third category of leadership is thankfully very rare nowadays. One may simply term it as inadequate. Security has become a way of life. Such leaders fear their insecurity. They are left with enjoying a status to which they adhere for their own salvation: they use the post not for what can be done for others but solely for themselves. In such schools good teachers become worse and if they have sense they leave. In the end only those either at the beginning or at the very end of their careers are left in such schools. Such leaders do not recognise anything but the temporary glorification of their own position.

## Qualities of leadership

Among the leadership qualities in effective schools - and these qualities can be found collectively in the senior management team - the following recur: being cheerful and optimistic even in adversity; showing welcome; obviously enjoying the achievements of others especially amongst all the staff and not just the teaching staff; being a good listener; taking the blame and showing fallibility; being able to see time in perspective and being able to organise that in relation to the various constituents; having a fairly well thought out philosophy and understanding of the differential nature of change.

Lastly, you will recognise the effective school by its appearance. It will be environmentally - but especially visually - aware. In this, of course, schools are blessed for better or worse by their natural inheritance; few can be better placed than some of the famous schools in the private sector. Nevertheless all effective schools make the best of their circumstances, even those in less promising ones, by using the internal walls and the background of the school as an additional subliminal factor. Schools for years have displayed children's work but the nature of that display will tell the perceptive visitor much about the effectiveness of the school. Does it, for example, represent a range of work from different children? Does it support the school's policies and practices across the whole range of the curriculum - maths, science, language as well as art and craft? Are there unfinished pieces of work, problems unsolved, puzzles to pose questions? Are the images reflective of the school's set of beliefs on the family, the role of women in society, for example?

There is a multitude of questions to ask when entering the school. A responsible and confident school often lets the pupil speak for it in showing visitors around, in answering the telephone and in welcoming a visitor at a school entrance which will be clearly marked. Some schools have gone further. There has been a conscious attempt to overcome the institutionalised feel of the school by the use of carpet, material and the abolition of the pervasive bell. In one instance it was even noticed that a school occupied its non-lesson time with orchestral, choir and other musical practice in the main thoroughfares of school activity. Noise as well as appearance affects the quality of learning.

So will the visitor, especially the professional visitor, with half an observant eye recognise the effective school: by its shared values, its treatment of one another, its cheerful leadership, its appearance and perhaps by the small talk of a staffroom where people exchange opinions about pupils, papers on the curriculum, and share ideas from the professional journals. Such evidence lies outside the lessons where the quality of the student's learning can be assessed. But how are such schools achieved?

## PROCESSES WHEREBY SCHOOLS BECOME EFFECTIVE

It has already been remarked that the effectiveness of a school is closely related to the quality of its leadership. Such leaders have to be chosen and the responsibility for that process rests on the local education authority and the governing body in a balance of partnership which is laid down by the 1986 Education Act. Once appointed, headteachers need to be valued and supported, through induction and appropriately timed periods of in-service refreshment, during the tenure of their office.

The school's leadership - the wise headteacher ensures as wide a sharing of this function as possible - will give early attention to collective processes of self-evaluation, sometimes drawn from the concern of staff and the wider community itself. Shared vision for the school is gradually established. Self-evaluation will be a tool to keep under review the match of declared principles to actual practices not only in the curriculum but in the school's organisation.

A visual policy for the school, for example, is maintained only by hard work and a systematic scheme in which all share. Particularly impressive recently was the example of one secondary school which had involved almost a quarter of its pupils and staff in devising different strategies for changed display in the public parts of the school.

## Processes of school organisation

The effective school does not ignore the bits and pieces of administration. One very famous headteacher remarked 'I take my stand on detail.' This will lead the effective school to list all the various administrative tasks and functions from their beginning to their end and to identify alongside each the person who is responsible for worrying over the timely completion of the various tasks being undertaken by others, but which collectively will lead to the successful completion of the operation. It matters not at all whether the task is a regular news-sheet to parents, a parents' evening, a play, a collection of option choices, a careers convention or a duty roster.

The effective school gives careful attention to its system of assessing the pupils' work. It is essential that the staff compare children's work amongst themselves in order to moderate and calibrate their own perceptions of standards and expectations of achievement so that they are not too low or too high. They must take care not to depend on norm-referenced marking systems but to make sure that marking is a further means of 'conversing' with the pupil. It is unlikely that teachers professing to be child-centred will be true to that belief unless they can demonstrate that they mark the children's work both in a timely fashion and in a way which is positive.

The principles of assessment in the effective school have informed the requirements of the Oxford Certificate of Educational Achievement (OCEA). They provide a set of principles as applicable to primary as to secondary schools for they will stimulate schools - their teachers, parents and pupils - to devise explicit maps of learning and chart the progress of all students in their journey of learning. They will have a policy for homework which is understood and followed by pupils, staff and parents. The involvement of these in a shared contract of learning can often be established whether in a survey or project work or in the attention to revision and further practice of examples. Parents can help enormously with memory tasks and practices established to foster mental agility, besides of course being supportive, understanding, giving of their time and trying to enable youngsters to have interesting experiences whether close at hand or far away from the home.

The school will typically have a set of expectations by which all agree to abide; a sanctions system will be understood and administered with sensitivity to the circumstances of the individual. The organisation of pupils in groups, classes or sets is closely examined to avoid inevitable expectation of failure and negative self-image which can result from streaming by ability in a general way. Nor should it be thought that such arrangements are to be found exclusively in the secondary sector where forms of setting based on interest and aptitude according to task, information and skill are again necessary as the youngster grows older; the colour coded tables in a reception class may have within them the seeds of future problems. The school gives close attention to its practices of consultation with parents, recognising their capacity as prime educators in their own right.

The last major process of achieving school effectiveness lies in staff development policy and practice. It will of course apply to all staff whether teachers or not and will range from an adequate system of induction (which should lead naturally to a form of individual personal review of plans and discussion of the realisation of those plans without all the paraphernalia and difficulty of an appraisal scheme) through to ensuring adequate time for personal reading, development and further training. There will be great care to differentiate between a collective staff development plan and that of the individual.

## Indicators by which a school judges its effectiveness

The school evaluation process has revealed a wealth of

measures - collections of evidence if you like - by which effective schools assess themselves. It will range from scores in tests of, for example, reading and mathematics, to the number and quality of school performances and events. There will be a check, pupil by pupil, on the opportunity for residential experience and involvement in service to the community and outside. Attendance rates of staff and pupils alike will be monitored. When it comes to examination results the school, with an eye to each youngster's achievement, will monitor not just the proportion of youngsters in the age group year on year getting higher grades, but the score per pupil over a range of subjects. The local educational authority may seek to compare schools of differing backgrounds. However, it is more important for each school to set up its own indices of performance in order to build ever higher achievement over the years.

## Role of the LEA

The role of the LEA in the process of achieving school effectiveness is complex but important. It includes, of course, the provision of adequate resources but it also covers much more. The LEA can set a climate and exercise its duties sensitively to stimulate the questioning, developing, self-confident school. It will tolerate individually different practices within a framework of principles; it trusts and praises in public but will vigorously 'police' in private rather than vice versa. Above all an LEA can create a professional and communal climate in which schools are more rather than less likely to be effective. Such an LEA will find its staff sought by others and it will publish its practices nationally. It will be particularly careful in its appointment procedures. It will have support service personnel - whether administrators, advisers or development officers - who demonstrate in their actions their understanding and encouragement for the subtle nature of change in schools.

The challenge to the LEA in this task has now become more formidable. It will be tempting, but wrong, to copy central government's top-down activity on the curriculum. Indeed, the advisers in particular will be busy acting as consultants or brokers to hard-pressed schools which must deal with the ill-timed incursions of Whitehall into the curriculum. Unless they are assisted, our effective schools will be undermined or overwhelmed by such activity which inevitably will interrupt the carefully considered development plan which is the feature of any school that has justifiable claims to effectiveness.

## Effective schools and government policy

The government in the early part of 1987 took a significant wrong turning in its educational policies. The signs of it were there in the 1986 Act with its last minute accretions such as the requirement for headteachers and governors to take account of the Chief Officer of Police when drawing up curriculum statements and in other clauses on matters such as political indoctrination. What these sections revealed was a government which was intent on general legislation as a result of particular and isolated incidents. Hence a few failing inner-city schools and one or two local education authorities failing in their task were dealt with, not as they might be through decisive intervention by the Secretary of State using his existing powers under the 1944 Act, but by punishing all schools and all local education authorities.

No matter that the standards of achievement are improving faster in the United Kingdom than in any other western European country. 'Spare us the facts, just feed our prejudices' seems to be the principle on which future educational planning is to be based. Hence the proposals for tests at seven, eleven and fourteen to ensure as the Prime Minister said (Torquay 1987) not merely that 'we are clear what children should learn but that we are sure that they are actually learning it'. The dangers of tests so far as school effectiveness is concerned are too obvious to mention. The pupils are either standardised by reference to the average performance of an age group thereby causing teachers to attend to those close to the average; or are differentiated so that youngsters become labelled early and perform according to that expectation. One director of education has actually spoken of holding children back a year in order that they should master the subject matter of the test. A sideways glance at the United States will reveal the logical outcome of these processes. There, they have such problems in their inner-city schools that armed police stalk the corridors and the cream of a generation cannot be tempted at any price into teaching. Teachers themselves in the United

States confess that they cheat when their students take the tests, either by giving their children more time, or by asking if they really meant to give that answer, or simply by doing the questions for them. It has all the inevitably of mediocrity of the Revised Code in the latter part of the nineteenth century. In the United States, for all their fine words about integration of children with special educational needs, they stop short of mainstreaming as a result of their strict adherence to age and grade.

Central government in England and Wales, with its promise of city technology colleges, its determination to allow popular schools to escape the system and its espousal of assisted places, not to mention tests related to age, demonstrates that it does not believe in the right of all children to enjoy a place in an effective school. For the structure it plans requires there to be at least three categories of school to which I have earlier alluded. The implications for all children with special educational needs are too obvious to emphasise. They are doomed to grace and favour treatment but are most likely to be in the state-maintained 'division-three' schools that will be created by the new arrangements.

Such a system, if indeed it is created, will last as long as the fissured society it creates does not erupt. It will simmer like a city perched on the continental shelf waiting for the inevitable earthquake - creating its ghettoes, ever-widening the gap between the rich and the poor, paying through the nose for its intolerance and increasing the size of its police force. It will, moreover, reverse half a century of development towards a different set of values.

## REFERENCES

DES (1977) Ten Good Schools, London: HMSO.

Galton, M. and Simon, B. (eds) (1980) Progress and Performance in the Primary Classroom, London: Routledge & Kegan Paul.

Rutter, M., Maugham, B., Mortimore, P., Ousten, J. and Smith, A. (1979) Fifteen Thousand Hours, London: Open Books.

# 2 WELFARE AND NEEDS IN SECONDARY SCHOOLS

Neville J. Jones

## INTRODUCTION

In the preface to the book Schooling and Welfare (Ribbins, 1985), Philip Taylor draws attention to the link between welfare and responsibility. He notes that 'schooling is one of the activities of a good society' and that 'it is one way among others of providing for the welfare of the people'. He goes on to point out that 'the processes and pre-occupations of schooling have not always ensured that the welfare of those in school is catered for in any direct and positive way'. If welfare is to be a positive activity then who has the responsibility to promote and carry it out? It is here that there is a wide range of disagreement among those responsible for welfare provision in our schools.

First, we may question whether a corporate body, such as a nation state or school community, has an obligation to establish welfare services. In doing so we can ask whether such a responsible act becomes qualified because of the different motives that are used by different political groups to justify the welfare response. In the period after the Second World War we saw the setting up of the Welfare State in Britain based on the recommendations of the 1942 Beveridge Report. This report was based on three principles: a range of proposals that, while taking into account sectional interests, should not be restricted by such interests; second, that there should be an attack on want, disease, ignorance, squalor and idleness, through social insurance, as part of a comprehensive policy of social progress; and third, that in a partnership between state and individual, the former would offer security 'for service and contribution' by the latter. The aim here was to secure a national minimum but to leave room for individual enterprise to live above the minimum.

What would be the parallels if these principles were applied to welfare in education? First, there would be the need to provide a welfare system that could be utilised by all pupils, as of right, and the service would not be organised only to meet the needs of a select few.

Second, the style of its universality would be that, in utilising the provision, pupils would not be at risk of discrimination, segregation or loss of pride or self-esteem. This touches on the way attitudes to need and disability are developed within a school, the way the welfare resource is located in the curriculum, and whose task it is to promote and carry out welfare duties and obligations.

Third, the welfare response must be handled in such a way that it comes to be regarded as a partnership in action between teacher and parent for the general wellbeing of the pupil. This may be difficult to achieve because welfare is a many-dimensioned activity ranging from the distribution of material help, matters of discipline, support for pupils in their learning, the making available of information on a wide area of topics, and counselling for careers as well as on personal matters. Furthermore, it is provided by a range of professionals, all of whom have both a personal ideology about welfare matters, and a professional set of values derived from their professional training and orientations. Some professionals are clearly comfortable in their welfare 'role' and carry out their work with welfare objectives and goals clearly in mind; others would not regard themselves as welfare providers, in any respect, even if their work had as an outcome a welfare dimension. Sometimes this is a very personal matter of how an individual regards him or herself in terms of professional identity. Certainly, this issue is one that constantly surfaces for teachers when they are called upon to carry out duties which they regard as 'social work' rather than pedagogic.

In spite of these uncertainties it is remarkable how extensive is the welfare network linked to schools, if welfare is used in the sense of being a response for the good and wellbeing of pupils in school. We need only refer to the list of professional titles below, which is not comprehensive, to see how far the network permeates a school quite apart from those who visit schools from support or community services:

- teaching staff: headteacher, year and department head; class and subject teacher; tutor; learning support teacher; careers teacher;
- within school staff: school counsellor; classroom assistants and welfare helpers; office staff, technicians, caretakers and cleaners;
- LEA peripatetic support services: specialist advisory teachers; youth and community workers; educational psychologists;
- social work: education social workers (ESWs); Social Work Department staff; intermediate treatment; psychiatric social work;
- medical services: family doctor; school medical officer (and consultant services); paramedical: school nurse, health visitor, audiometrician; therapist (speech, physio, psychotherapist).

The above has not included the police juvenile bureau, school governors and elected councillors and parents, all of whom at some stage in a pupil's time at school may become involved and known to the pupil's teacher.

The term welfare is not so commonly used these days, being associated with poverty and unemployment of the years between the two world wars, and in educational contexts has largely been replaced by the term 'pastoral care'. We can consider recent developments in respect of pastoral care in schools and attempt to appraise how far these services meet the criteria for the existence of appropriate and responsible welfare, for example, as set out in the Beveridge Report.

## PASTORAL CARE

Much of the planning for the Welfare State took place in the 1940s. Pastoral care was until the late 1960s a fairly marginal activity in schools but pressure to institutionalise it came with the publication of a number of books such as Marland's symposium Pastoral Care (1974). It is not, perhaps, coincidental that pastoral care began seriously to develop as a feature of schooling at a time when secondary schools were moving towards comprehensivisation between 1955 and 1965. The size of these new institutions was beginning to give rise to fears about their management, how large groups of pupils were to be controlled, and how the essential relationships for learning could be secured and maintained between teachers and their pupils. Very soon a division of interest and activity began to emerge between matters related to subject teaching, mainly the core curriculum, and others related to, and supporting, subject learning. This latter activity included the keeping of records, the dissemination of information to students, links with parents, homework, maintaining discipline and associated punishments, and generally coping with pupils who became disaffected and alienated from much of the conventional work and values in a school.

The large schools offered a wide range of choices for students and these were linked to future examinations and post-16 education. This was accompanied by increasing awareness of the social and personal problems that students experienced and how these could be responded to in a more organised way than dependence on individual teacher initiative. A response to both these aspects grew with services in schools for educational, vocational and pastoral counselling, coupled with the development of skills to cope with student needs on an individual basis.

The 1970s were a period when pastoral care began to make inroads into what might be called the formal curriculum of a school. In the first place students were being introduced to a range of skills and understanding to make their own individual learning more effective. These were not just study skills but those of making and sustaining effective relationships with others. The field began to widen beyond that of personal, social and moral education, linked to tutorial work in groups and courses on 'life-skills', to areas such as careers, health and sex education. These trends in the way the pastoral care activities were beginning to make a charge on curriculum resources were recognised by HMI (1979) in their publication called Aspects of Secondary Education.

The closer these activities became allied to the central curriculum concerns of a school, the greater the demand on teachers with a pastoral responsibility to develop new expertise, knowledge and skills within a framework of 'active learning' approaches. Towards the end of the 1970s a plethora of publications appeared both from government sources and from LEA innovations. The Further Education Unit at the Department of Education and Science published Experience, Reflection, Learning (1978), A Basis for Choice (1979), Developing Social and Life Skills (1980), Beyond Coping (1980), and Tutoring (1982). In 1978 Hamblin published The Teacher and Pastoral Care and Hopson and Scally (1979, 1981) Lifeskills Teaching Programmes Numbers 1 and 2.

Central to the pastoral activity was the work of the group tutor (Blackburn, 1975) whose task it was to:

- care for pupils as whole persons, i.e. in relation to aspects of the pupils' life at home, school and in the local community;
- record and monitor attendance and problems like absences and punctuality associated with school attendance;
- monitor progress and initiate change when this is seen to be required;
- offer educational and vocational advice, utilising specialist help within the school and by LEA advisory services, on option choices, further education and employment;
- interpret school policies to pupils;
- link parents and the school.

In recent years the activity of pastoral care, within the context of the role of the tutor, has been in a more formally structured curriculum practised under the title of Active Tutorial Work. The Active Tutorial Work programme developed out of a Lancashire LEA in-service programme in the mid-1970s. The adviser for education in pastoral relationships was actively involved with a county policy that set in train a major in-service training programme throughout Britain. These courses were led by Douglas Hamblin, well-known for his work at the University College of Swansea on pastoral care and counselling (1974, 1978, 1981, and 1984), and by Leslie Button (1981 and 1982). Also involved, as group leaders, were two Development Officers, Jill Baldwin (Blackburn) and Harry Wells (Burnley).

At this time Leslie Button was involved in a number of LEAs working on a project funded by the Leverhulme Trust 'which involved testing models of developmental group work and established a team of trainers for such work'. Arising from this activity a curriculum development study was mounted to devise 'a teaching programme for pastoral work aimed at facilitating the pupils' growth and development through their own active experience'. East Lancashire released sixteen teachers to assist with this work which extended for a day a month for two years. The study involved both an in-service programme for teachers and the compiling of programmes and materials which could be used in schools for 11- to 16-year-old pupils. Materials compiled and tested were published between 1979 and 1983 under the title Active Tutorial Work Books and were designed as a 5-year programme of pastoral work for use in tutorial periods by staff in comprehensive schools (Baldwin and Wells, 1979-1983). During this period of development of Active Tutorial Work the Health Education Council funded at Bristol University a one-year evaluation study (Bolam and Medlock, 1985).

Certainly by the early 1980s it was becoming clear that a strong pastoral care movement was going to emerge within what Ribbins (1985) has described as 'an influential, much used, yet essentially shadowy concept employed to account for and justify a variety of more or less compatible purposes and practices within the contemporary school'. If it is true that pastoral care is becoming as pervasive as is being suggested then it is likely to influence areas of schooling beyond those of making a response to discrete groups of pupils whose needs arise because of social disadvantage, deprivation, disturbance or disruption. If schools both reflect the culture of the society in which they exist and are the proving grounds for the development of skills to equip pupils for a post-school labour force, then we might expect pastoral care in its wider dimension to play a greater role in relation to matters such as community participation, work and unemployment, as well as leisure (Watts, 1983). Pring (1984) has raised questions about teacher responsibilities and the extent to which they have obligations towards the social welfare of pupils as part of the wider but central concern of education. This has become a central issue revolving round what is known as the pastoral-academic split.

## UNIVERSAL WELFARE

Disagreements about the place of pastoral care in schools, and the extent to which some or all teachers should be engaged, is to some extent a reflection on the process whereby welfare in schools has gradually become institutionalised. Until some two decades ago pastoral functions, largely centred round discipline issues, were considered marginal to the main aim of the educational process. It was argued then, and is still a view put forward today, that caring activities are not the prerogative of all teachers but require a very special kind of personal empathy and skill. Put simply, this argument maintains that it is not possible for an individual teacher to exercise what might be considered to be a control function and yet combine this with a caring and pastoral approach. This seems a very weak argument even if it were true and is an odd commentary on the role of parents who combine, and find no difficulty in combining, a wide spectrum of caring and disciplinary roles. What was more to the point was that some teachers did not regard pastoral work as within the domain of professional teaching and it was administratively convenient for there to be a division of labour on these matters. Hence the pattern of services that emerged was for a separate pastoral service with pastoral posts linked to individual teachers, tutors and year heads. But pastoral concerns, allied with comprehensivisation of schools, soon extended to counselling and group work, and eventually to what was being called the 'pastoral curriculum'. Pastoral care was gradually infiltrating areas of school life that before had been the preserve of others. Expectations grew that all teachers would exercise a pastoral as well as an academic role. But there were anxieties among those working in the pastoral field about this tendency towards universalising pastoral functions. Heads, and others, began to take a stand on these matters.

Shepherdson (1983), headteacher of a large comprehensive school in London, took the view that pastoral care was no more than 'an administrative convenience', a non-existent phenomenon, because all teachers have very distinctive roles which embrace the range of skills that come under the term 'pastoral care'. Shepherdson argued against dividing pastoral and academic roles and functions because:

- some teachers try to take on the role of the doctor, social worker or psychologist, with all the attendant dangers of amateurism or straight bungling;
- to do so is to set up an invidious notion that some teachers 'care' while others do not;
- pastoral teachers are seen as second-class citizens by other teachers and by pupils.

To this extent, therefore, Shepherdson was not supportive of the setting up of the National Association of Pastoral Care in Education (NAPCE) in 1982 and the publication of a new journal under that name. This was 'a sad development which simply perpetuates the idea there are some people with a special skill'.

The emergence of a new 'institution' in education, like NAPCE, resurrects again the issue of how a society responds to a need, and whether that response is in the form of some kind of positive discrimination. The kind of growth in pastoral care services, though over a much shorter time scale, has been similar to the way services for pupils with special educational needs have grown and become institutionalised. The first step is always in the identification of a group of pupils with needs; this brings into existence a range of activities and organisational procedures aimed at doing this in the most efficient and economical way. The growth of school psychological services in this country is testimony to this kind of institutional mushrooming. Very soon everything becomes 'specialist' or specialised: teachers, qualifications, equipment and buildings, support staff, advisers, administrators, research and government policy - all eventually to be inspected by HMI with a special brief. The whole process discriminates - in favour of pupils either to or against their advantage, and against ordinary teachers who become de-skilled in many areas where they already have knowledge and expertise but no brief to practise.

It takes very little time for organisational considerations to outweigh the reason why the system was institutionalised in the first place for the needs of pupils. In 1986 the National Executive Committee of NAPCE published a Position Statement in relation to In-service Training for the Pastoral Aspect of the Teacher's Role, recommending in mirror-image all the institutional aspects now seen with the other organisational system, special education. The danger is not so much in the advocacy of making an appropriate response to a given need, but the way this response is orchestrated. Too often this is done through procedures that further handicap the clients because of management strategies that segregate or stigmatise. This invariably happens when needs are handled outside normal responsive processes and pupils regarded as a special case for whatever extra help is required. We have yet to see in Britain a legalisation of rights that ensures for those in need a protection against bureaucratic interventions which, of nature and kind, only serve to set some individuals apart because their individual needs are in some degree not those of the majority. Titmuss (1968) expressed the problem in another context i.e. in relation to state welfare services:

> The real challenge resides in the question: what particular infrastructure of universalist services is needed in order to provide a framework of values and opportunity bases within and around which can be developed socially acceptable selective services aiming to discriminate positively, with the minimum risk of stigma, in favour of those whose needs are the greatest?

Best (1983) defends the split between academic and pastoral functions on the grounds that there is a specific task to be carried out - the converting of the caring into effective practice - and he takes the view that not all teachers can acquire all the necessary skills. Marland (1974) makes the same point when he says (p.11) that 'it really is a truism of school planning that what you want to happen must be institutionalised. It is not enough to rely on goodwill, dedication, hard work, personality and so on...' There are, of course, many ways in which corporate enterprises can be institutionalised and the criticism of Marland's point of view is that the way present-day pastoral care services are organised in schools is one among many styles of school management that are capable of bringing about the same or similar results.

A parallel situation can be found in the way LEAs responded to the provisions of the 1981 Education Act. Already an extensive professional bureaucracy existed for the management of special education. The 1981 Act became a trigger for extending this in the appointment of a large number of additional educational psychologists, mainly to cover the paper work for completing the 'statementing' procedures. Similarly, most LEAs have appointed an adviser for special educational needs i.e. category posts for the administration of services largely in the segregated sector, instead of subject-orientated posts. This has been done to improve the quality of the service provided by the LEA for pupils with special educational needs.

There is little evidence that extending bureaucratic services ever improved the quality of services at the customer or client level. Within school management at the moment there is ample expertise and knowledge, on both good management and effective teaching, to bring about better opportunities for those with special needs without the special procedures set out in the 1981 Education Act. It has been argued that additional 'specialist' posts have been created, out of pressures created by the 1981 Act, as a way of encouraging lethargic LEAs to improve their standards. There is no guarantee that this will happen, partly because many professionals regard the 1981 Act provisions as irrelevant to their work in schools, and consequently have little or no incentive to make an extra response. It is also true that lethargic LEAs are likely to be authorities where pupils with special educational needs are segregated and marginalised from mainstream interests.

Similar kinds of question might be asked of pastoral care in its present form as a service to schools separate from other school activities. Is it necessary to create new structures when what is required can be achieved in so many other ways? A possible reason for the independence of the pastoral care services in a school is that their actual independence signals to others that their purpose and place is to service those parts of 'normal' schooling that are not working well. Another way of looking at this is to say that by providing the extra response to a small number of pupils they allow the majority of pupils and teachers to pursue their work uninterruptedly. This allows pastoral care to remain educationally neutral. No questions are asked of the school as a whole, no changes expected, and no enquiry is made as to the extent to which the patterns of management and teaching actually contribute to some of the problems of pupils who receive certain kinds of pastoral care.

There are those who actively promote a neutral approach and would regard this as a wise policy: there are many publications on pastoral care which in their advocacy of practice sustain a position of neutrality (Blackburn, 1978; Johnson, 1980; Best, 1980; and McGuiness, 1982). This general position has been summarised by Best (1985, p.22). The aim here is to set out a detailed list of 'prescriptions for a school seeking to improve its pastoral provisions without threatening the school's right to go on existing in a fundamentally unchanged form'.

It might be questioned as to whether pastoral care has got itself precisely into the position of not being able to challenge what happens in some of our schools because of its insistence on being a service independent of other school activities like subject teaching. Clearly, not all welfare responses are to circumstances and conditions that are bad in schools, but it is worth remembering that with systems that do not work well, and may in outcome produce the conditions requiring welfare, to make the provision may be no more than to perpetuate what the welfare in its final goal aims to remove.

The kind of issues discussed above in relation to pastoral care in general also create difficulties for specialist practitioners who provide a specific kind of service. This has been the case with the development of counselling in schools.

## COUNSELLING

So far there has been no satisfactory resolution to the question as to whether a school should employ a full-time trained counsellor or whether counselling should be regarded as a set of skills to be developed by all teachers. There is little doubt that some of the received wisdoms inherent in the training of professional counsellors can also be part of the repertoire of skills that all teachers, from time to time, need to call upon. These central skills apart, a decision has to be made as to how much time is to be given to the counselling welfare that is provided for each pupil, and whether for some pupils the need is for more time than can possibly be provided by class teachers. We can consider briefly some possible roles for the specialist counsellor, the role that such a person might play in relation to the broader pastoral care functions of a school, and consider what skills are intrinsic in the counselling approach which all teachers might find of use in their daily teaching roles.

Counselling has increasingly become recognised as a skilled activity involving a relationship between counsellor and pupil and utilising a range of skills for the purpose of allowing the counselled individuals to take some positive action in their own interests.

Counselling has been defined in a broad sense in the following terms:

> A purposeful and enabling relationship in which individuals learn to understand themselves and their environment better, and how to handle their personal development, their roles and their relationships with other people. (Jones, 1986)

To this extent counselling is an interactive process which does not confine itself to the work carried out by specialist counsellors, but has a developmental aspect aimed at increasing awareness and growth, both for individuals and groups. Although counselling skills are involved in the work of careers officers their task is different from that of counselling per se in that a high element of advice-giving constitutes part of the aim of the interview. Advice-giving is studiously avoided in the counselling contract.

Because counselling can be a highly personalised activity, opening up a range of confidences, there has to be negotiated from the beginning the rules for confidentiality. This aspect of counselling has to be delineated from the wider view of counselling as an activity that threads itself through a range of school activities like tutoring, guidance, staff development and other aspects of pastoral care.

Counselling is a set of skills drawing upon a range of disciplines, such as psychology, sociology, social anthropology and educational philosophy, and from which a range of strategies and approaches have developed. As an applied social science, with counsellors either opting for a specific model of work or drawing in an eclectic framework on many theories and disciplines, counselling has become a confusing activity in schools. But in spite of this those who counsel have in common many areas of approach and technique. The counselling task is seen quite clearly as one in which pupils are to be helped and for this to be done by way of a determined method of negotiation. Although a counselling exchange may take place in other than a 'therapy' room, such as a school corridor, counsellors sensitive to their role will never treat the exchange of views as a cosy chat or just an excuse for someone to unload tensions. There is an actual process of clarifying individual issues and feelings. There is a third stage where decisions are made as to what actions are to be taken for the continued process of the counsellor and pupil working together. These decisions are about the structural framework in which the counselling task is to proceed and not decisions that arise from the counselling interchange which remain the responsibility of the pupil.

Counselling, to be effective, requires that the counsellor has a critical perception, one that can be developed through professional training, of self-behaviour and its impact on others. Wylie (1980) has listed three aspects of behaviour, related to individual personality, which he considers to be helpful to the counselling task:

- the ability to 'feel into' a person - the ability to take, for the purposes of counselling, his or her standpoint or perspective upon affairs, the ability to grasp the implications of events for them and them alone. This is known as empathy;
- to be genuine. There is no place for trying to put on a false front, for a pseudo-professional relationship which places technique above being genuinely human. One has to search for a congruence between what one says and what one feels: for the feelings will, in the end, show through - in the way we sit or raise our eyebrows or in the tone in which we speak;
- the capacity to show warmth: to indicate that we care and that we believe in the student's ability to do something about the problem.

These three essentials have been expressed in other terms as follows:

> The process of counselling involves the application of a variety of specific skills: for example listening, reflecting back, clarifying of ideas, empathising, picking up non-verbal signals, developing an understanding of what is happening in the exchange.
>
> The climate of a counselling session and the relationship should be neither threatening nor judgmental, but rather should foster trust, self-awareness and personal growth on both sides. (Jones, 1986)

Some LEAs have pursued a specific policy of appointing specialist counsellors in their schools, but this is still exceptional, and the climate of falling rolls with financial cut-backs has not encouraged the expansion of specialist posts. Furthermore, some heads of schools have tended to regard counselling as an intrusion into their own areas of pastoral jurisdiction. Counselling has too often been offered to schools as a mystique. Teachers have sometimes felt undermined in their own professional roles and been critical of specialist counsellors as having a relatively privileged and stressless occupation.

Counselling within a school is sometimes offered as a very specific service for the benefit of a few pupils in need, or to relieve pressures on class teachers where pupils are disruptive or emotionally disturbed. In such systems the referral procedures are carefully controlled, usually through tutors, and pupils have no rights to the service as in the case of schools which organise 'drop-in' approaches or self-referral. Systems of counselling where the flow of clients is carefully controlled, and where the orientation to the counselling task is likely to be towards regarding the problems as 'within' the student, are not likely to give rise to a questioning of school structures, teaching skills and teacher-pupil relations, all of which may have contributed to the pupil's need for help. In some respects such a model of counselling mirrors the system of pastoral care where the welfare response has been separated from the teaching function.

A school, therefore, seems to have open to it one of four options:

- not to have a specialist counsellor but to encourage all teachers to develop as far as possible counselling skills;

- to appoint a trained counsellor and for teaching staff to concentrate specifically on their pedagogic roles of teaching formal curriculum. Here students may or may not have choice of access to the counselling service;
- to appoint a trained counsellor who combines a counselling function with teaching duties;
- to appoint a trained counsellor who would work with students but also has a wider brief in terms of providing service to other staff in the school in more direct ways than in the support provided to students.

In schools where there is no full-time counsellor then the task covered by a specialist counsellor falls either on the shoulders of class teachers, or is taken on by tutors by virtue of the pastoral system, or is met through the utilisation of other agencies such as the school welfare officer or school educational psychologist. We have seen that a specialist counsellor working to a system that regards student problems as student-centred carries the risk that there will never be an end to some kinds of problems because their roots are in the school system as experienced by the students. It is a problem shared with those who advocate a separate system of pastoral care. Counsellors who are also teachers appear to be in roles of expediency and it is not easy to be clear about the efficacy of this type of school management.

It has been argued that a school counsellor fulfils the most positive role when working with students, within the wider pastoral network of the school, and with subject teachers. This allows the counsellor to deal with those problems which arise from outside the school, as with family crises, as well as with 'within school' matters. It allows a better integration of the work of the counsellor into the wider framework of pastoral care, and as such may help its recognition and legitimacy. In this respect the counsellor can be supportive to quite a substantial range of matters which affect class teachers. These include:

- establishing systems of referral within schools, with outside agencies, and clarifying criteria for such referrals;

- providing consultative support to pastoral care staff in their work with students;
- increasing the repertoire of skills which tutors require;
- linking with parents where there has been a breakdown of liaison between teacher and parent;
- reviewing the record-keeping of a school and its assessment procedures;
- reviewing teaching programmes and methods in relation to individual need;
- providing the extra time needed to unravel the problems which some students have.

These examples show that if the counsellor is not careful then this role can easily become a jack-of-all-trades post. Some of these activities lie clearly and appropriately within the job description of the ordinary class teacher. But the class teacher cannot meet these needs when the timetable and teaching commitments are such that they are left undone if not picked up by someone with the time and disposition to do them. It is questionable whether all this is the rightful role of the school counsellor.

It may be in the nature of an effective welfare service that responds to the diversity found with human problems that no single theory, methodology, system of management, can be universally uniform. It does not, however, help the cause of counselling when counsellors offer a variety of approaches, ideologies and skills, so wide that headteachers are confused as to how to utilise their skills to the advantage of a given school. The diversity may to some extent account for the range of expectation from headteachers and the fact that some heads find the accommodating of counselling methods and practices too difficult to bother with. In such circumstances headteachers will often look outside the resources of the school to support services like educational social work and school psychology.

## EDUCATION SOCIAL WORK

Education social workers were originally known under the 1870 Education Act as 'attendance officers'. They were employed by the School Boards but did not lose their 'school-board man' image when the Boards were abolished by the 1921 Education Act. Since 1944, the title education welfare officer has been used. The Education Welfare Officers National Association (EWONA) changed its name in 1977 to the National Association of Social Workers in Education (NASWE). The changing name has reflected the developing role and function of education social workers, from school attendance officer, to education welfare officer, and now to education social worker. It is only in recent times that the profession has begun to claim a firm stake in the social work field and to cover a wide range of duties related to social work and schools. There is possibly an urgent need now for education social workers, in the light of the Government's Circular 2/86, to make a firm claim to be regarded as and called social workers who work in education. This may need to be underpinned by a determined effort on the part of the profession to ensure that all its members are qualified in teaching or social work, or both.

The change in the role of the education social worker has been slow and is in some measure a reflection of change in attitudes to the social and educational needs of pupils at school. This has to be seen as part of the historical shift from when pupils were first required formally to attend school in order to create a literate population able to meet the needs of commerce and industry, to more recent times when the nature and quality of education provided has become part of the stated rights of children in society. This changing philosophy towards children's educational needs has found expression in a number of reports that have been published since the mid-1960s (Plowden, 1967; Seebohm, 1968; Ralph, 1973; Warnock, 1978; and the more recent House of Commons Inquiry into Children In Care, 1984).

These reports have given added support to the claim that educational social workers are now in the forefront of social work with children in our schools. The scope of educational social work in Britain today is given some indication from the following brief list of activities:

- enforcing the bye-laws relating to the employment of juveniles;
- children in entertainment;
- provision of educational social benefits;
- pupils with special educational needs and their families;

- pupils with behaviour problems linked to truancy and non-school attendance;
- pupils inappropriately placed in ordinary schools who face suspensions and sometimes expulsion;
- provision for expectant schoolgirls;
- discovery and involvement with child abuse cases;
- escort duties;
- taking school population censuses.

Additionally there has in recent years been an extensive programme of research into ways in which classroom management and school organisation can affect pupil behaviour towards both conformity and disruption (Hargreaves, 1967; Lacey, 1970; Ball, 1981). These studies were part of a movement in educational research away from looking at issues of equality and opportunity, which considered social class background and school achievement (Halsey et al., 1961; Craft, 1970), to a study of relationships within schools. This did not mean, however, that home factors, particularly in relation to social deprivation and disadvantage, were no longer an area of legitimate research (Brown and Madge, 1982; Lodge and Blackstone, 1982; Mortimore and Blackstone, 1982). Research in America had focused attention on how pupils perceive the way their teachers treated them and how this determines subsequent pupil deviance (Werthman, 1963).

Following the early studies by Hargreaves and Lacey, a number of studies looked at how pupils made sense of their school experiences and interpreted the behaviour of teachers (Gannaway, 1976; Rosser and Harre, 1976; Beynon, 1984); the way pupils negotiate with teachers, the rules of the classroom and the amount of work they are prepared to do (Ball, 1980; Woods, 1978); and pupil relations with each other in terms of leadership, friendship patterns and gang behaviour (Hargreaves, 1967; Davies, 1982; Pollard, 1984). Other researchers have linked classroom behaviour and school management back into family cultures, particularly pupils from working-class homes, suggesting that the 'conflict' that develops 'normally' in classrooms is not so much a function of a group dynamic, with pupils and their teachers, but a counter-cultural phenomenon in schools when working-class pupils find themselves taught by teachers with middle-class values (Willis, 1977; Corrigan, 1979; Anyon, 1981). New research is also emerging on the effects of gender and the way this is shaped by family socialisation, teaching, pupil cultures and how they contribute to differentiation in the curriculum, and life chances generally (Deem, 1980; Stanworth, 1983; Measor, 1984); ethnic issues (Fuller, 1980); and school effectiveness (Reynolds, 1985).

These reports and research studies in linking home and school have not only pinpointed sources of difficulty but indicated how we might go about preventing, managing and remediating in respect of pupils who during their school years become alienated from schooling. Because behaviour problems, and needs generally, may have their roots in any one or more of the sources now being researched, a new perspective is placed on the role of those in the welfare areas of school activity. The balance of explanation at the present time for pupil behaviour that is in some way deviant is centred in looking at the interaction dynamics of pupils with their experiences at school, or the way they perceive such interactions. This opens up the possibilities for change to take place and for all who work in schools to be part of the change process. As with international charity to Third World countries, those with welfare or pastoral functions may need to question whether their work styles, and methods of intervention, actually place a brake on change.

Education social workers could be well placed to take an important role in such change processes in schools, linking as they do the school and the home. Somehow the management of pupils with needs, behavioural or otherwise, must be focused towards a professional group who are well placed to take into account both school and home factors. The opportunity came recently to exercise some imagination in this field when the government decided to review the work of the education social work service. All that it could achieve was to see education social work in its 1880s dimension of being a service to catch truants and to ensure that children attended school. It was a view that found support from the National Association of Schoolmasters and Union of Women Teachers. To all other unions, educational organisations, and professional groups familiar with the work of education social workers, the approach taken by the government was unacceptable and no longer reflected events that had taken place in the education social work service over the past twenty years or more.

## Educational psychology

Educational psychology in schools has passed through a number of phases with different emphases in terms of skills offered, the purposes of intervention and efforts to offer schools welfare support. Initially recruited for the purposes of selecting out pupils for special education, utilising methods of the now increasingly devalued psychometrics, school psychologists have from time to time reintroduced behavioural techniques to aid learning, explored a systems approach to school organisation and engaged in therapeutic interventions with pupils and families. All these approaches are still utilised by school psychologists and may possibly account for the confusion in the minds of many teachers as to what to expect from their school psychological service.

It is unfortunate that at present there is no coherence about school psychology as this is experienced by teachers nor, indeed, a collective view among school psychologists as to their purpose and function. Part of the difficulty is that, professionally, school psychologists are pulled in two directions: towards the psychology espoused as a behavioural science, which has little application to the day-to-day work of teachers in schools, but provides for some psychologists a semblance of professional respectability; and towards schools and education, where they secure for themselves employment and a career. School psychologists have never made up their minds whether they are first and foremost psychologists in the 'scientific' tradition, who happen, among a variety of job opportunities, to have opted to practise their skills and expertise in education, or whether they are essentially educationalists who draw upon their training in psychology to advise and determine their contribution to work in schools.

In the former situation psychologists distance themselves from an accountability within the education service, partly in a belief that this secures for them an independence essential for their work; but this helps to sustain certain myths about what psychologists can and cannot achieve. It also means that school psychologists cannot expect to have the support, or indeed the protection, of educational interests in the development of a psychological service within education. Headteachers become quite angry with the way school psychologists negotiate what they will do, how, when and in what manner, in the service they offer to schools. If school psychologists are serious in their intention to be considered as experts on school matters, then almost the first thing they will have to do is to give up pretensions to being scientists, and to recognise that most of what happens in a school, when done well, is highly skilled. A second requirement would be for school psychologists to explore the area of partnership, offering and expecting a role of mutual working with other educationalists, in a variety of educational settings. There is a need for psychologists with graduate qualifications to be employed in schools as teacher-psychologists long before such individuals move towards a specialist training in educational psychology. The present system of graduate psychologists being employed first as teachers - thus abandoning their professional identity for as long as it takes to reach the number of years set down by training organisations before they can return to being psychologists - is confusing.

Although educational psychologists are dissatisfied with their role as 'test technicians' they are very reluctant to give up this area of their work. It is unfortunate that at a time when educational psychologists were seriously considering other more profitable ways of using their skills, and moving away from psychometric testing in its various guises of pupil assessment, LEA school psychological services were burdened with the largely irrelevant demands for assessment under the 1981 Education Act. Educational psychologists have ventured into the field of school management, for which they have usually had no personal experience, little relevant training and no invitation from heads of schools to carry out such work. The lack of credibility of school psychologists stems partly from the fact that until as recently as twenty years ago there were few educational psychologists employed by LEAs and it makes no sense to talk of a service as if it had a history of regularity and continuity. But educational psychologists are also faced with a reality about schools and what they are about, namely, that they are places of continual change. Whereas some twenty years ago it might have been expected that pupil assessment would be carried out by some expert other than the class teacher, this is no longer the case. Development in the area of pupil profiling, the extension of teacher in-service schemes, the need for teachers to respond to pupil needs where there has been an integration policy regarding the disabled, have all meant that it is the teacher in the classroom who is, and should be, the expert on assessment procedures. This is no longer the central domain of the educational psychologist. It provides an opportunity for educational psychologists to reappraise their work in schools and to develop skills that would be of more relevance with the school as the starting point for a psychological practice rather than a psychological laboratory.

Some extremely useful exploration of these issues took place towards the end of the 1970s resulting in the publication of two 'reconstruction' books which looked at changes within the structure of school educational services at that time (Gillham, 1978; McPherson, 1981). During 1986-7 a group of psychologists and educationalists met to explore what kind of psychological service might be developed, if the starting point was that of the school, and what decisions have to be made daily in schools covering all aspects of management and teaching. This would be a psychology of schooling having a different theoretical base and practice from a psychology that is not bounded by the canons of natural science. The publication that has emerged from these discussions can only offer tentative solutions, being a contribution to what must ensue as a literature on transition, but its essence is to suggest a way forward rather than to set out any dogmatic prescriptions (Jones and Sayer, 1988). Changes, whatever these might be, have to be owned by those who are likely to be most affected should they take place, but in this book it is suggested that ownership should be in educational hands and this means partnership of educational psychologists and others working within education.

## SUMMARY

In this chapter we have looked at the general concept of welfare in schools, expressed through institutionalised pastoral care, and considered specifically in specialist services within schools. These services include counselling, education social work and educational psychology. Welfare in education has been related back to certain principles that were first worked out as part of the planning of national services leading to the setting up of the Welfare State in Britain in the period following the Second World War. These are principles related to whether a welfare response should be universal, as a question of individual rights, or a selective service following a policy of 'positive discrimination' for minority groups; the problems of selective welfare which easily create other problems related to stigmatisation; and the right of individuals to a service that is not in essence benevolent charity. A central issue related to all forms of welfare, whether as charity to Third World countries, or state welfare, or pastoral systems within schools, is whether the welfare response itself does little more than secure the continuance of the conditions that created the welfare need in the first instance.

## REFERENCES


Anyon, J. (1981), 'Social class and school knowledge', Curriculum Inquiry, 11.

Baldwin, J. and Wells, H. (1979-83), Active Tutorial Work, Books 1-5, Oxford: Basil Blackwell.

Ball, S.J. (1980), 'Initial encounters in the classroom and the process of establishment', in Woods, P. (ed.), Pupil Strategies, Beckenham: Croom Helm.

———— (1981), Beachside Comprehensive, Cambridge: Cambridge University Press.

Best, R., Jarvis, C. and Ribbins, P. (1980), Perspectives on Pastoral Care, London: Heinemann.

Best, R. and Decker, S. (1985), 'Pastoral care and welfare: some underlying issues', in Ribbins, P. (ed.), Schooling and Welfare, Basingstoke: Falmer Press.

Beynon, J. (1984), ' "Sussing out" teachers: pupils as data gatherers', in Hammersley, M. and Woods, P. (eds), Life in School, Milton Keynes: Open University Press.

Blackburn, K. (1975), The Tutor, London: Heinemann.

Brown, M. and Madge, N. (1982), Despite the Welfare State: Studies in Deprivation and Disadvantage, London: Heinemann.

Corrigan, P. (1979), Schooling the Smash Street Kids, Basingstoke: Macmillan.

Craft, M. (1970), Family, Class and Education: A Reader, London: Longman.

Davies, B. (1982), *Life in the Classroom and the Playground*, London: Routledge & Kegan Paul.

Deem, R. (1980), *Schooling for Women's Work*, London: Routledge & Kegan Paul.

Department of Education and Science (DES) (1967), *Children and their Primary Schools* (Plowden Report), London: HMSO.

______________ (1978), *Report of the Committee of Enquiry into the Education of Handicapped Children and Young People* (Warnock Report), Cmnd 7212, London: HMSO.

Department of Health and Social Services (1968), *Report of the Committee on Local Authority and Allied Personal Social Services* (Seebohm Report), London: HMSO.

______________ (1973), *Role and Training of EWO's* (Ralph's Report), London: HMSO.

Fuller, M. (1980), 'Black girls in a comprehensive school', in Deem, R. *Schooling for Women's Work*, London: Routledge & Kegan Paul.

Gannaway, H. (1976), 'Making sense of school', in Stubbs, M. and Delamont, S. (eds) *Exploration in Classroom Observation*, London: Wiley.

Gillham, B. (1978), *Reconstructing Educational Psychology*, Beckenham: Croom Helm.

Halsey, A.H., Floud, J. and Anderson, C.A. (1961), *Education, Economy and Society*, London: Free Press.

Hamblin, D. (1974), *The Teacher and Counselling*, Oxford: Basil Blackwell.

______________ (1978), *The Teacher and Pastoral Care*, Oxford: Basil Blackwell.

______________ (1981), *Teaching Study Skills*, Oxford: Basil Blackwell.

______________ (1984), *Pastoral Care - A Training Manual*, Oxford: Basil Blackwell.

Hargreaves, D. (1967), *Social Relations in a Secondary School*, London: Routledge & Kegan Paul.

Johnson, D., Ransome, E., Packwood, T., Bowden, K. and Kogan, M. (1980), *Secondary Schools and the Welfare Network*, London: Unwin Educational.

Jones, E. (1986), *Counselling: a Discussion Paper* (HMI Working Paper), London: DES.

Jones, Neville J. and Sayer, J. (1988), *Management and the Psychology of Schooling*, Basingstoke: Falmer Press.

Lacey, C. (1970), Hightown Grammar: The School as a Social System, Manchester University Press.
Lodge, P. and Blackstone, T. (1982), Educational Policy and Educational Inequality, Oxford: Martin Robertson.
Marland, M. (ed.) (1974), Pastoral Care, London: Heinemann.
McGuiness, J. (1982), Planned Pastoral Care: A Guide for Teachers, London: McGraw Hill.
McPherson, I. and Sutton, A. (eds) (1981) Reconstructing Psychological Practice, Beckenham: Croom Helm.
McPhail, P. (1982), Social and Moral Education, Oxford: Blackwell.
Measor, L. and Woods, P. (1984), 'Cultivating the middle ground: teachers and school ethos', Research in Education, no. 31.
Mortimore, J. and Blackstone, T. (1982), Disadvantage and Education, Studies in Deprivation and Disadvantage, London: Heinemann.
Pollard, A. (1984), 'Goodies, jokers and gangs', in Hammersley, M. and Woods, P. (eds) Life in School, Milton Keynes: Open University Press.
Pring, R. (1984), Personal and Social Education in the Curriculum, London: Hodder and Stoughton.
Reynolds, D. (1985), Studying School Effectiveness, Basingstoke: Falmer Press.
Ribbins, P. (ed.) (1985), Schooling and Welfare, Basingstoke: Falmer Press.
Rosser, E. and Harre, R. (1976) 'The meaning of trouble', in Hammersley, M. and Woods, P. (eds) The Process of Schooling, London: Routledge & Kegan Paul.
Shepherdson, I. (1983) in Rogers, R. The Caring Bit, TES, 25 February 1983.
Stanworth, M. (1983), Gender and Schooling, London: Hutchinson.
Titmuss, R.M. (1968), 'Welfare state and welfare society', in Commitment to Welfare, London: George Allen and Unwin.
Watts, A. (1983), Education, Unemployment and Future Work, Milton Keynes: Open University Press.
Werthman, C. (1963), 'Delinquents in school: a test for the legitimacy of authority, Berkeley Journal of Sociology, 8, pp. 39-60.
Willis, P. (1977), Learning to Labour, London: Saxon House.
Woods, P. (1978), 'Negotiating the demands of schoolwork', Journal of Curriculum Studies, 10, pp. 309-27.

Wylie, T. (1980), Counselling Young People, Leicester: National Youth Bureau.

# 3 WHOLE SCHOOL POLICIES: A QUESTION OF RIGHTS?

Caroline Roaf

## INTRODUCTION

Certain assumptions, not hitherto based on serious study, have been made about whole school policy. As a phrase it has generally been thought to mean very little in itself and attention has concentrated instead on the topic raised as the subject of a whole school policy rather than on whole school policy as a concept in its own right. While teachers are aware of a considerable range of topics commonly the subject of whole school policy-making, such as multi-cultural education and special educational needs, and may have considerable experience in the implementation of these, when asked what they think a whole school policy is in general and what demands it might, in general, be expected to make on them and the institutions they run, they are less interested. To the general public, which includes parents, governors and politicians, the phrase is, as yet, unfamiliar.

In this chapter I want to challenge this lack of interest in whole school policy as a concept in its own right. I want to suggest that, on the contrary, its study, by encouraging us to look for connections between different areas of whole school policy making, sheds light on an important, but so far somewhat obscure, aspect of education. I hope to be able to show that by examining the notion of whole school policy in general we can isolate a particular group of policies which share a central concern with human rights. They are, therefore, not only of great public interest and significance in themselves, but also because understanding them and the way they interact is essential if we are to understand much that is problematic in the management of special educational needs.

## BACKGROUND

For a phrase which has been used and is being used with so much enthusiasm and which is of such potential significance, it is remarkable that the first article to treat the subject as a generic term appeared in mid-1985 (Boyd). It has not found its way into dictionaries of educational terms, nor is it a useful term when conducting a computer search, or in scanning works such as the British Education Index. This came as something of a surprise since the phrase has been increasingly in use since the late 1970s. The Bullock Report (1975), with its phrase 'language across the curriculum', seems to have prepared the ground in which the concept could be developed, as indeed it was.

> Coherence in a school does not necessarily mean integrated areas... it means instead that, whilst each aspect of work in a comprehensive school should be encouraged to be different, to retain its special contribution, there should be properly worked out agreements amongst the staff on a number of 'whole school policies'. (Marland, 1977)

Although not actually used in the Warnock Report (1978) itself, the groundwork for such an approach and phrase in the special needs context is clear, particularly in the chapter on special needs in ordinary schools and the chapter on the curriculum.

> Such an outcome (integration) will not occur spontaneously. Nor will it be achieved by legislation alone. It has to be contrived and patiently nurtured. It means greater discrimination in favour of those children with special needs, in proportion to the severity of their disabilities. The planning, initiation and sustaining of integrated education calls for considerable knowledge, skill and sympathetic dedication by everyone concerned - parents, teachers, administrators and other professionals of different kinds. (Warnock Report, 7.11)

Another area in which to pursue the matter of whole school policy is in the literature related to particular client groups: in case studies of schools, in such areas as pastoral care, multi-cultural education, language development or special educational needs. In much of this literature, where a whole school policy is implied, though the term may not actually be used, it is rare for one policy to be seen in the context of any other. Since an attempt to develop a whole school policy in one area of the school can easily be defeated by the operation of other policies in other areas, this reluctance to look for interconnections provides further evidence of the lack of understanding of whole school policy with which we are concerned.

One particular feature of client group studies which is of great significance to the study of special educational needs and is related to whole school policy has been the way in which concepts such as 'learning difficulty', 'cultural diversity' and 'social disadvantage' have interfered with each other in teachers' perceptions of their pupils' abilities and potential. The confusion resulting from this has caused great injustice to many groups of children and has been well documented (Barton and Tomlinson, 1981) and has been stressed in both the Rampton (DES, 1981) and Swann (DES, 1985) Reports. These confusions are recognised in the Warnock Report:

> There is no cut and dried distinction between the concept of handicap and other related concepts such as disability, incapacity and disadvantage. Neither is there a simple relationship between handicap in educational terms and the severity of a disability in medical or a disadvantage in social terms. (para. 3.3)

A telling example is the case of Travellers' children. Are they multi-cultural or special needs? What is really implied by each of these terms? The literature is thus intriguing as much for what it does not say as for what it does and for the insights which are not noticed and connections not made as for those which are. It is in order to avoid the confusion of attitudes towards both special needs and cultural diversity, and the waste of energy which arises from this, that we need to explore the idea of whole school policy more thoroughly. Having done so, we need to relate it to the management of the curriculum itself, to the way in which access to it is controlled, and to the method by which it is delivered in the classroom.

## TOWARDS A DEFINITION

What then is understood by the term whole school policy? In the absence of any recognised definition, this is a challenging question. In a recent (1985) DES short course on Pupils with Special Needs in Ordinary Schools, attended by administrators, advisers, support staff and teachers from all over the country, among the papers circulated to course members was the following statement and series of questions:

- A whole school policy on 'learning difficulties' is regularly advocated by HMI and many others. But what is such a policy? Does anyone have one at present and what should be its purpose?
- What aspects of school life are currently covered by whole school policies? Exams and assessment? Anti-racist policies? Corporal punishment?
- What should be the aims of a whole school policy on learning difficulties? To identify problems? To prevent them? To remedy them?
- What features of school life should change? What should be the components of the policy?
- Under what conditions can a whole school policy on learning difficulties be introduced? How can a whole school policy be developed and accepted?
- Would a whole school policy conflict with other policies and practices?

In fact, although the conference, on its final day, settled down to produce plans for a whole school policy on children with learning difficulties, these plans were made without any satisfactory attempts to answer the prior questions. This experience reinforces what interviews and school visits also reveal, that, although increasingly used, whole school policy is a phrase so far without clear definition and that the significance of this omission has not been grasped.

We have, therefore, to begin at the beginning. It helps, before discussing what the words 'whole school' add, to start with the word 'policy':

- any course of action adopted as advantageous or expedient;
- a definite course of action selected among many alternatives, to guide and determine future decisions;
- a high level overall plan embracing the general goals and acceptable procedures.

Using these definitions in the school context we can see, first, that schools are governed by a large number of different policies. Some have become so much a part of what schools are, in the popular imagination, that they are no longer perceived as policies. Pupils take examinations, follow certain curriculum patterns, receive regular reports on their work, schools run parents' evenings and so on: these are all matters of policy - easily ossified, however, and overlaid by tradition, convention and habit. Furthermore, educational policies operate in many different and interlocking areas, both within and outside the school, and within the practice of individual teachers.

Beyond these fairly elementary considerations we have to consider some more far-reaching implications. Inherent in the idea of policy is the implication of change, of growth and development and this is reflected in the phrase 'selected... to guide and determine future decisions'. More important is the fact that policies are usually presented as aims with objectives. We have to be able to distinguish between those that tend towards a 'good', and are tied to an acceptable principle, and those that are merely 'advantageous' or 'expedient'.

## POLICIES AND PRINCIPLES

The relationship between policy and principle is an intricate one, particularly since few schools are able to start from scratch. It is much more common for a school to use policy to modify and determine principle and to influence the future development of ethos in that way. The problem has been, particularly in the development of comprehensive schools, that there have been so many uncertainties not only within the teaching profession itself, but also among the politicians and civil servants who provide and resource them, as to what principle educational policy in these schools was supposed to be based on anyway. Circular 10/65 was all about organisation. Precious little was said then about principle, let alone the principle of equal value, and nothing at all about what this actually meant in terms of the nature of, or access to, the curriculum. Yet it is precisely because of the way in which thinking on these matters of principle has developed in the last twenty to thirty years that we are now so concerned to develop holistic responses to issues which are seen to challenge our understanding of the principles on which our education system operates. In arriving at a definition of whole school policy we have, therefore, no choice but to digress briefly on the matter of principle.

The chief ground for believing in the equal value principle is that of justice: 'No-one shall be presumed, in advance of particular cases being considered, to have a claim to better treatment than another' (Peters, 1966). Distinctions may be made if there are relevant differences but not otherwise, thus putting the onus of justification on the person wishing to treat someone else differently. In what circumstances is it justifiable, for example, to remove a child from an ordinary school into a special school, or vice versa? How do we ensure that gains for some should not be at the expense of losses and disadvantages to others? Clearly, then, there are a lot of different factors intruding here - cultural, social and political; it is not my purpose to pursue these, rather to assert that if these principles of social justice are important at all, they are doubly important for children.

From this brief digression and discussion of principle, one becomes aware of much greater complexity when returning to the question of policy. This is the assumption that policy, as with principle, will be arrived at by processes of rational argument and by working towards goals which, when achieved, will become part of the school's ethos - something to be introduced, discussed, modified and absorbed, and in so being, to 'modify and determine future decisions'.

By tacking on the words 'whole school', what do we add? There is the obvious supposition that the policy is something applying, and understood, school-wide. But the way in which the phrase is actually used, and the policies to which it has become attached, suggest something much stronger. Policies on multi-cultural education, equal opportunity or special educational needs are deeply rooted in attitude change. They are thus qualitatively different from many other policies, such as a policy on whether to teach SMP maths or traditional maths. Both are different from policies to abolish school uniform, which, although it may modify behaviour could, arguably, be undertaken by a school without any profound change of attitude on the part of the teachers. Yet both could be said to be 'whole school'. We are thus immediately aware both of the complexity here in the link between behaviour and attitude and that we may find it helpful to develop a typology of whole school policies.

## A DEFINITION

So far, then, we can sum up by defining - for the moment and bearing in mind that we may wish to modify it in the light of some kind of classification - a whole school policy as a policy clearly understood by the whole school community, whose purpose is to guide and determine the ethos of the school and to support attitudes and behaviour consistent with that ethos.

When asked about the educational purpose of whole school policies, one teacher had this to say:

> A whole school policy is a way of raising issues and feeding in information. People are often stumped about what strategies to use to raise the issues. For example, multi-cultural education is a difficult issue and difficult to raise, especially in all-white schools. It's a way of making teachers know and feel what the concerns are that these issues are supposed to be responding to. It's very important for teachers to be part of the process.

In this quotation we can discern three main interlocking intentions: a whole school policy which heightens awareness of a particular issue; a whole school policy which offers a strategy for bringing this awareness about; and that this awareness be supported by an input of information.

By referring to our definition, we can see that this

adds considerably to our understanding of it. We can now say that a whole school policy, by providing a platform from which to reiterate principle, encourages teachers to think more deeply about the nature of the educational enterprise they are engaged in. Ultimately then, the purpose of a whole school policy is to modify the school's ethos, organisation and management, to the benefit of the children's education, by raising consciousness and changing attitudes.

## ISSUES

There is more to it than that, however. First, it is by no means the case that all examples of whole school policy attract so much serious or extended consideration as seems to be implied in these definitions. Second, we already seem to be focusing on the word 'issues' and these, as we know, frequently arise as a result of external pressures of one kind and another. They rise and fall on a school's policy making agenda according to the pressure of the moment.

The idea that there are issues to be concerned about in education has been around for a long time. The issue of education for girls is one, as is the education of the handicapped, and the concept of 'secondary education for all'. However, these issues, particularly those to do with educational opportunity and achievement, have usually been in the context of groups who had been denied an education, particularly a secondary education, of any kind. It was assumed that, once they had the opportunity to go to school, that was the end of the issue. Any subsequent underachievement was therefore seen as either psychogenic or sociogenic. It is a relatively recent phenomenon for educators in general - there have always been a few pioneering spirits - to begin to recognise that teachers' attitudes, reflected in their behaviour, methods and in the structure of the organisations they run, are intimately connected with the level of achievement of their pupils. A succession of major reports - Bullock (1975), Warnock (1978), Swann (1985), and the major ILEA reports, Hargreaves (1984), Thomas (1985a) and Fish (1985b) - all carry the same underlying message. Any discussion about the purpose of whole school policies must stress, therefore, their importance as a means of educating teachers.

## INTERCONNECTIONS

Having decided to treat whole school policy as a generic term one can learn a good deal more about the concept by examining the inter-relationships between two issues commonly introduced as whole school policies. For the present purpose the examples of multi-cultural education and special educational needs are particularly useful. Both these subjects have a long and involved history of developing ideas and a background in social, economic and political history. In both there has been a considerable time-lag between the development of the concepts and their translation into practice and both have emerged as issues about which educators and others say, 'It's time we had a policy on...', thus introducing the element of expediency which is so characteristic of policies in general.

By using the two major government reports, Warnock (DES, 1978) and Swann (DES, 1985), as 'witnesses' to the nature of both issues and looking closely at what is implied by each, we find that they have certain kinds of activity in common. Both set out:

- to examine society's attitude and behaviour towards specific groups of children and consider questions of prejudice and discrimination; and
- to examine the needs of these specific groups of children; their needs as individuals and their needs as members of identifiable groups.

In other words, by focusing on these two issues as examples of whole school policy we also seem to have drawn attention to something else: that these particular policies are basically concerned with human rights and that needs arise where there are violations of those rights. To what other policies are they then related and what are the implications of this?

Human rights issues abound but gender and class are of particular importance in education along with race and handicap, each of which have been the subject, as we have seen, of separate government inquiry. There are, of course, other candidates, such as ageism and localism - children develop intellectually, physically and emotionally at different rates and to different levels. Children from certain housing estates or localities suffer varying forms of prejudice and discrimination and there are plenty of cases where the rights of individuals are violated. If we restrict our inquiry simply to race, gender and handicap, it will come as no surprise to find that these are all characteristically the subject of whole school policies.

## HUMAN RIGHTS POLICIES

The idea that there is a group of policies which could be called human rights policies, each with the dual purpose we have outlined, is in fact a very accurate reflection of what is actually happening in relation to race and gender. This takes us to the heart of the confusions which have arisen over the phrase 'special educational needs'. Although tensions have existed between multi-culturalists and anti-racists, there is now recognition in many quarters that they are both necessary, and complementary, parts of the same policy. The same is true in the case of gender and would, we may now assume, be true over any issue involving violations of rights.

If we take four of these - gender, race, class and handicap - we can see that violations of rights in any of these areas will need provision special to that area to redress them, and that this provision should be made in the context in which the need for changed attitudes and behaviour, and a changed environment, is fully recognised. Moreover, we can see that meeting the special needs of, say, a black, working-class, handicapped girl requires four different, yet interconnected kinds of action, some of which may involve physical/pedagogical provision and others attitudinal, some to be met within a school and some in the community. A human rights view enables one to see each issue separately but acknowledges that they frequently interact and that class, not - as with gender, colour or some forms of handicap - so readily identifiable, frequently interacts with them all. It also brings handicap back into the picture, but in a new way in which attitude change is placed on an equal footing with the provision of resources. For the mentally handicapped some might think this emphasis was long overdue.

## SPECIAL EDUCATIONAL NEEDS

The confusion, which we noted earlier, over the use of the phrase 'special educational needs' seems to have arisen because a phrase which we actually need for use on a much wider front was appropriated by and became firmly attached to the Warnock Report which was about the abolition of categories of handicap. The case for loosening this connection is strong and has become even more forceful as we increasingly stress (see, for example, Fish, 1985) both the notion of 'equal opportunities for all' and the relative nature of handicap itself. In fact, Warnock's development of a new view of special education did hint at this:

> much broader and more positive... it encompasses the whole range and variety of additional help, wherever it is provided and whether on a full or part time basis, by which children may be helped to overcome educational difficulties, however they are caused.

It did encourage a new way of thinking about children's needs, but it is one which has been dominated by the vested interests, and inertia, of those whose professional interests were primarily concerned with handicap.

The 1981 Education Act moved the matter on significantly in section 1 subsection 4 which states that:

> a child is not to be taken as having a learning difficulty solely because the language (or form of the language) in which he is, or will be, taught is different from a language (or form of a language) which has at any time been spoken in his home.

By appearing to acknowledge that some children may need special provision, although they do not have learning difficulties, this curiously worded paragraph (What children are being referred to? What is meant by 'form of language'? Non-standard English? Dialect?) makes an important distinction which is taken up in the Fish Report. This distinguishes between 'special educational need' arising from learning difficulties and 'special need' arising from factors other than learning difficulty, yet both requiring special provision. It is, in practice, a distinction, given the increasingly relative nature of handicap, which is hard to make and hard to respond to since the holistic response to a person's needs which we now espouse requires a careful analysis first. The previous emphasis on learning difficulties, and the special provision required to meet the needs arising from these difficulties, has meant that we have been blinded to the fact that we should have been addressing ourselves first to issues which are essentially human rights issues, and only then to questions of need.

A specifically human rights perspective can, I believe, help us analyse needs and develop more effective strategies for meeting them in two important ways. Such a perspective sees needs as arising wherever there are violations of rights. The emphasis and focus of attention are less on individual children, who cannot be held responsible for their environment, or the attitudes and behaviour of those among whom they live, than on that very environment and those attitudes. It should, therefore, help to remove some of the burden of guilt and stigma which is still the lot of children who are deemed to have special educational needs. It should similarly help teachers distinguish more clearly between the needs they can reasonably be expected to meet in school and those which are properly the responsibility of society. Once this is clear, the responsibility for redressing violations of rights can be more clearly apportioned.

## SOCIO-ECONOMIC CLASS

In spite of the general reluctance to use the word or concept at all, the question of socio-economic class is worth considering at this point. It is generally known, for example, that children whose parents are in socio-economic groups 5 and 6 (as defined by the Registrar General) are more likely to be in bottom sets, leave school early, appear in court, have poorer life chances and, more serious still, be the subject of a special educational provision geared to the needs of a group with which they may have little in common whether in the mainstream or special school. This, as operated at present, is in itself having unfortunate results. 'All the world over, powerful social groups are in the process of categorising and classifying weaker social groups, and treating them unequally and differentially' (Tomlinson, 1982); and again:

'Occupational succession, social mobility, privilege and advancement are currently legitimated by the education system; those who receive a "special" rather than an ordinary education are, by and large, excluded from these things' (ibid). The relationship between being a member of a weak social group with consequent lack of opportunity, and being in receipt of special educational provision implying something demeaning and stigmatising, is painfully close and tells us much about our attitudes to those who are disabled. Once again we are faced with a situation which is essentially one of attitudes and rights. Whatever improvement has come about in recent years is partly as a result of better resources, but even more because of changed attitudes, so that those who suffer from some kind of impairment, and as such have learning difficulties, are less restricted.

Socio-economic class is almost always mentioned or alluded to in some way, however indirect, in other policy statements on human rights issues. We find it in Swann (1985), and Warnock (1978) and in many of the case studies and client group studies (Ball, 1981). We also find it being used, as in Oxfordshire, as an 'indicator' when determining the allocation of extra staffing to schools: not on the basis of numbers of children with learning difficulties, as perceived by the schools, but on the basis of criteria such as the number of houses with outside lavatories, no running hot water, number of people per room, proportion of households headed by someone born in the New Commonwealth and single-parent families. It thus provides us with many interesting examples of the way in which those responsible for provision do in fact try to break the bonds placed on us by the historic and habitual association of the term 'special needs' with 'handicap'.

## IMPLICATIONS FOR MANAGEMENT

Turning to the implications for the management of these human rights policies we need to go back a step, and recall that in identifying a certain type of whole school policy as being concerned with human rights, a classification of whole school policy was implied. Looking then at the range of possible whole school policies, we find that very broadly speaking some are primarily the concern of pastoral care groups, and some of curriculum groups. In spite of the obvious overlaps between them, these two groups each have organisationally distinct structures responsible for the formulation, planning and management of policy. Department/faculty meetings and tutor/year/house groups fulfil these necessary functions.

If human rights issues constitute another area of policy making, what structures are there whereby they can be formulated? In most cases there are none, largely because the need for such a structure has not been perceived. Some schools, it is true, are now beginning to develop policy-making bodies, with titles such as 'standing committee' or 'policy group', and some schools have created posts in which the post holder has a clear responsibility for a human rights issue. But these are still very much the exception, and even in schools which have a policy-making group, there tends not to be any particular system for prioritising or ranking the policies it develops. Nor is there any system for making the necessary connections between the different policy-making areas nor for interconnecting the policies made within each area. Thus a whole school policy on, say gender, can be implemented independently of any other policy, either in its own area, for example, race or handicap, or in a different area, such as pastoral care.

There are two further problems. One is the ease with which schools confuse policy-making with executive and administrative functions.

> Just as administration and leadership get muddled up, so do the executive structures of an organisation and its policy structures. All organisations need a structure as well as people to exercise the leadership function, that is, to decide direction, priorities and standards and to take the precedent-setting decisions. This is usually called the policy structure. They also need a structure divided into various roles and responsibilities, whereby people are charged with the responsibility for a piece of action. This is the executive structure. (Handy, 1984)

The second is the sheer difficulty of the policy-making process. From what has been said earlier about the nature and purpose of policy, and its close link with something as potentially contentious as 'principle', one is able to understand exactly how demanding both emotionally and intellectually the task of policy making is, and how easy it is for powerful vested interests to operate within this process. This is not, perhaps, surprising but simply reinforces the need for structures and planning.

It is only when we have got to grips with a definition and typology of whole school policy that we can begin to decide, first, what particular areas of activity are likely to be associated with each type and, second, what particular groups of people should be represented on each policy-making body. Since we have already established the link between human rights policies and special needs we will remain in that area for the present purpose. If we accept that principle cannot be translated into practice without reference to policy making, and further, that it is the human rights policies that give expression to the principle of equal value, then I think we can begin to identify some of the most important matters of concern to this policy-making group. Chief among these will be questions of access to the curriculum, the formation of teaching and tutorial groups, the organisation of special provision in relation to the major human rights areas, the consideration of individual human rights and certain other matters such as the content of the school prospectus, the system of rewards, community links and appraisal. It is also likely that the members of such a group will need to be representative of the whole school community and that therefore one will expect to see members of both the teaching and support staffs as well as representatives from the parent and governing bodies serving on it.

## NEW CONTEXT FOR SPECIAL EDUCATIONAL NEEDS

By chipping away at our notions of what it is to be handicapped, and by emphasising human rights, we find ourselves with a very different perspective of special educational needs. Needs, we find, not only arise from various kinds of disability, but also from violations of human rights.

These violations occur typically in certain clearly defined areas and, moreover, it is very frequently the case that individual children have needs which arise because they experience more than one kind of oppression. It is being recognised increasingly that these groups frequently overlap and that each requires resources and action special to it. The needs of girls, of ethnic minorities, of children in rural areas, of children who develop precociously and so on, must be met in different ways. It is not enough simply to declare that such and such a child has 'special needs' without asking to what issues these needs relate and how they interact. This perspective also provides a safeguard against the tendency, mentioned by Tomlinson, for 'powerful social groups' to categorise and classify weaker social groups and to treat them 'unequally and differentially'. It is only by insisting that powerful social groups acknowledge human rights that we can achieve any kind of equality.

The implication for special educational needs is, I believe, that if a human rights perspective is adopted, then it becomes apparent that special needs teachers need to have a very much more sophisticated idea of their brief than they commonly do. It will not be good enough to talk in an imprecise way about children with 'learning difficulties'. We will be concerned with the special needs which arise wherever human rights are violated.

Looked at in this way, it can be argued that much of what at present passes for a 'whole school policy on special needs' is no more than half a policy. Special needs of whom? Girls? Pupils with physical disabilities? Travellers' children? Or do we really care how children's needs arise? We have somehow, by abolishing the categories of disability, allowed ourselves to overlook causes. Thus it is possible for a school or district to declare, in a quite undifferentiated way, that it has such and such a percentage of children with 'special needs' - figures vary but can be anything between 20 and 80 per cent. They are not only thus unable to push for the resources they need in each specific area, but also give encouragement to those who attribute failure or underachievement to learning difficulty when in fact it is nothing of the sort. A more analytical approach can help schools synthesise, and make more effective, their strategies to meet needs. Being a 'special needs' teacher - and it will be important to work out what is meant by this in a new context - will in future mean not only knowing how to identify and meet needs arising from disability but also, by distinguishing between these and other needs arising from violations of rights, being able to become more efficient in the organisation of special provision and more effective in the defence of children's rights.

## REFERENCES


Ball, S.J. (1981) Beachside Comprehensive, Cambridge: Cambridge University Press.

Barton, L. and Tomlinson, S. (1981) Special Education: Policy, Practices and Social Issues, London: Harper and Row.

Boyd, B. (1985) 'Whole school policies', Forum for the Discussion of New Trends in Education, 27, 3.

Department of Education and Science (DES) (1965) Circular 10/65, The Organisation of Secondary Education, London: HMSO.

__________ (1975) A Language for Life, Report of the Committee of Inquiry (Bullock Report), London: HMSO.

__________ (1978) Special Educational Needs (Warnock Report), London: HMSO.

__________ (1981) West Indian Children in our Schools, Interim Report of Inquiry into the Education of Children from Ethnic Minority Groups (Rampton Report), London: HMSO.

__________ (1985) Education for All, Report of the Committee of Inquiry into the Education of Children from Ethnic Minority Groups (Swann Report), London: HMSO.

Handy, C. (1984) Taken for Granted? Understanding Schools as Organisations, York: Longman.

Inner London Education Authority (1984) Improving Secondary Schools (Hargreaves Report), London: ILEA.

__________ (1985a) Improving Primary Schools (Thomas Report), London: ILEA.

__________ (1985b) Educational Opportunities for All? (Fish Report), London: ILEA.

Marland, M. (1977) Language Across the Curriculum, London: Heinemann.

Peters, R.S. (1966) Ethnic and Education, London: Allen and Unwin.

Tomlinson, S. (1982) A Sociology of Special Education, London: Routledge & Kegan Paul.

# 4 GUIDANCE, COUNSELLING AND SPECIAL EDUCATIONAL NEEDS: MANAGEMENT AND CURRICULUM ISSUES

David Galloway

## INTRODUCTION

A school's responsibility for its pupils' pastoral care, and more specifically for their personal and social education, is not controversial. In the early days of free and compulsory education in Britain this was not, however, thought to have any important curriculum implications, nor was it considered necessary to develop an elaborate pastoral network involving all teachers in the school. Instead, in the smaller schools of the selective era, responsibility for pastoral care and for pupils' general welfare was centred on the headteacher and a small number of senior colleagues.

An analogous attitude prevailed in school policies towards special educational needs. Until the Warnock Committee produced its report (DES, 1978), it was widely assumed that only a tiny minority of children, perhaps two per cent, would require special education, and that this would be provided in a special school or class. Apart from some generally rather haphazard 'remedial' provision, special educational needs were simply not considered much of a problem for ordinary schools.

In Britain, many of the former grammar and secondary modern schools contained fewer than 250 pupils. With the development of larger schools in a comprehensive system of secondary education came recognition that guidance, or 'pastoral care' as it is usually known in Britain, must be placed on a more formal footing. It proved administratively expedient to do this by allocating each school extra financial resources to pay experienced teachers an enhanced salary for undertaking responsibilities in the area. Other education systems have responded differently, by appointing a trained 'guidance counsellor' to each secondary school, but this model never gained widespread acceptance in Britain (Murgatroyd, 1983).

It is doubtful whether the development of guidance networks was directly related to the growing recognition that schools were failing to cater effectively for the needs of a substantial minority of pupils. Warnock's recommendation that policy should be based on the assumption that up to 20 per cent of pupils would require some form of special education provision at some stage in their school careers reflects this recognition. So, from a rather different perspective, did the Hargreaves Committee's report in its comments on the education of pupils of below average ability in London secondary schools (ILEA, 1984).

This chapter will review the aims and scope of guidance activities in schools in order to discuss the management and curriculum implications both at national level and at school level. We shall then look critically at the evidence that up to 20 per cent of children have special educational needs, and again review both management and curriculum implications at national and at school level. Finally, we shall briefly consider the role of a school's pastoral care network and its pastoral curriculum in identifying and meeting special educational needs.

## AIMS AND SCOPE OF PASTORAL CARE

### Background

Few teachers would have much difficulty in accepting three propositions: that all pupils should feel that at least one teacher in the school knows them well; that recognised procedures are needed to ensure coordination and dissemination of relevant information affecting the educational welfare of individual pupils; that each pupil's progress should be monitored systematically across the curriculum.

These propositions all indicate the need for a pastoral network. One member of staff, such as a counsellor or deputy head, may have responsibility for coordinating this network but the person concerned cannot do the work himself. Nor is it realistic to delegate responsibility for each pupil's care to heads of year, known as 'deans' in some countries. In many schools, well over 200 pupils are admitted annually and it is unrealistic to expect one or two teachers to undertake personal responsibility for each of these pupils. For purely practical reasons, the basis for any effective pastoral network must be a team of form tutors. This is only feasible if it is acknowledged that most, if not all, teachers in the school should have responsibility for a tutor group in addition to their roles as subject teachers.

Whether teachers accept pastoral responsibilities may depend on how far they accept responsibility for the 'all round' development of their pupils. In theory at least, this responsibility is not controversial. Since effective discipline implies good personal relationships throughout the school it is hard to deny the school's responsibility for its pupils' personal and social education. The aim of this may be stated as ensuring that all pupils are seen, and see themselves, as contributing members of the school with a developing understanding of their rights and responsibilities, not only in the school but also in their families and in the community.

## Scope

It is clear that educational aims require planning. Whether the plans are systematised into a curriculum for personal and social education is a matter for debate, to which we shall return. There can be no dispute, however, that other aspects of pastoral care do require systematic attention in the curriculum. This is evident from consideration of the four major aspects of pupil pastoral care: provision of personal, social, educational and vocational guidance.

A common fallacy is to assume that educational guidance is concerned solely with advising pupils on choice of subjects for public examination purposes. Its scope is much wider, being concerned in the broadest terms with the pupils' effective use of the school. The relevance of this is seen in the demonstrably poor use which many pupils with learning and adjustment problems make of their school. Educational guidance, then, includes the induction programmes for newly admitted pupils, or pupils embarking on a new stage of their career in school, study skills, information retrieval and the ability to make informed choices of subject option.

Another fallacy is to assume that personal and social guidance will look after themselves if pupils can take their problems to a counsellor and/or if teachers take a sympathetic interest in their welfare and maintain effective discipline. In reality, personal and social guidance include health education, sex education, the ability to relate in a culturally appropriate way to people in authority and the social skills young people need if they are to play an active part in their school, family and community. Several subject departments in a secondary school may legitimately claim interest in health education or sex education, for example, PE, biology, religious studies and home economics. Yet without careful planning there is a danger that some pupils will miss out altogether and that others will receive unnecessary duplication.

A third fallacy is that careers education - a term with wider connotations than vocational guidance - does not start until a year or two before pupils expect to leave school. Yet educational choices have obvious implications for subsequent career choices. One wonders, for example, how many girls are aware of the career opportunities closed to them when they elect to take arts rather than science courses leading to public examinations. In addition, the skills required in making informed choices, such as the ability to seek and evaluate relevant information, are skills which form part of both an educational guidance programme and of a personal and social guidance programme.

## Terminology

The organisation and scope of pastoral care in a secondary school can be seen more clearly by defining some of the more commonly used terms. The pastoral network simply refers to the way the school organises itself to cater for its pupils' welfare. Hence, this is essentially an organisational concept with no inherent implications for the curriculum.

As we have just argued, though, the four major aspects of pastoral care each require systematic planning, and this does have curriculum implications. The pastoral curriculum refers to the facts, skills, attitudes and concepts which children need to acquire in order: to make the best use of the school; to promote their personal and social development; and to make informed choices about subjects and future careers. The content of the pastoral curriculum is beyond the scope of this chapter, but has been admirably described in a seminal article by Marland (1980). The pastoral programme refers to the school's arrangements for implementing the pastoral curriculum. Every major subject department bases its work on its own agreed curriculum, and produces a programme to show in detail how, when and by whom the curriculum will be taught. The same principle applies to the pastoral programme.

The tutorial programme refers to that part of the overall pastoral programme which is taught in tutorial groups by form tutors. It is important to note here that some aspects of the guidance programme will not be covered in subject departments. The part played by the subject departments as opposed to form tutors will vary from school to school. Ideally, transfer of learning will be facilitated by cooperation between senior staff responsible for the tutorial programme and heads of subject departments. Some study skills, for example, can be taught initially by form tutors and reinforced by subject teachers.

## IMPLICATIONS FOR EDUCATIONAL ADMINISTRATORS

### National level

An effective pastoral network will include most, if not all of the school's teachers. Moreover, it is difficult to envisage a satisfactory pastoral curriculum in which form tutors do not play an important part. These arguments may be considered in the light of policy in many countries to appoint full-time counsellors to secondary schools. The tensions and ambiguities in a counsellor's role in a secondary school have been discussed elsewhere (Galloway, 1985a). The important point here, though, is that counsellors seldom have the personal inclination, professional training or status in the school to act as coordinator of a pastoral network, let alone to develop a comprehensive pastoral curriculum throughout the school. Even when they do have the inclination, training and status, their credibility with their teacher colleagues is often low. Teachers are understandably sceptical about the ability of someone with no regular and substantial teaching commitment to provide professional training and leadership.

It is doubtful, then, whether the appointment of counsellors will do much to encourage effective pastoral care in schools. Indeed, a national or LEA policy to appoint counsellors may constitute an almost insuperable hurdle in developing a pastoral network. The reason is that the counsellor is seen as a specialist, trained to deal with pupils' problems. Consequently, students with problems are readily seen as the counsellor's responsibility. This tacitly encourages teachers to refer 'problems' to the counsellor. In practice, the problems they refer are disproportionately of a disciplinary nature. The irony here is that the group of pupils whose behaviour is least likely to change as a result of counselling are those who present problems of disruptive or anti-social behaviour (Levitt, 1963; Robbins, 1972; Mitchell and Rosa, 1981). More serious, if problem pupils are seen as the counsellor's responsibility, it requires no great logical leap for subject teachers to conclude that all other pupils in the school must be making adequate progress, and hence that guidance lies outside the ordinary teacher's regular duties.

If this argument is correct, the challenge for educational administrators at national and LEA levels is two-fold: to encourage schools to establish a guidance network which ensures that the needs of all pupils are recognised - we have argued that this must involve all or most teachers and be based on a form tutor system; and to develop a guidance curriculum which provides a practical basis for guidance activities, but is nevertheless sufficiently flexible to be adapted to the particular needs of each school.

The guidance network most widely adopted in schools in Britain is that in which there is a division between pastoral and subject curriculum responsibilities at senior management level. This does not facilitate incorporating the pastoral curriculum into the mainstream curriculum. The model does, however, show how all teachers can be involved in pastoral tasks. It implies that each teacher will be a member of a pastoral team, coordinated by a head of year, as well as of a subject team, coordinated by a head of department. It also implies, as Marland (1983) has penetratingly argued, that the principal function of the head of year is to provide professional leadership. In this model, it is logically as absurd to judge a head of year by his ability in counselling the more difficult pupils as to judge the head of maths by his ability in teaching them. The departmental head is judged by the quality of teaching throughout the department. Similarly, a head of year should be judged by the quality of guidance provided by the team of tutors.

Development of a pastoral curriculum requires encouragement at national level or, in Britain, at local authority level. At present there is a dearth of commercially available material. The most widely known schemes (Button, 1981; Baldwin and Wells, 1981) are based on a rather limited theoretical model, focusing on tutorial work rather than on the wider concept of the pastoral curriculum. Even as manuals for tutorial sessions their usefulness is limited. Instead of developing tutorial work from the tutors' existing skills as subject teachers, they tend to emphasise the differences between tutorial work and subject teaching. The effect is to arouse resistance among many teachers, particularly to aspects of the programme dealing with personal and social education. There is an urgent need for guidance to establish the aims and scope of the pastoral curriculum. Related to this, a programme of in-service education and training is needed to equip senior teachers with the knowledge and skills to implement it in their own schools.

## School level

Development of a pastoral curriculum and tutorial programme has implications for school organisation, in-service training within the school and classroom practice. Headteachers generally agree that form tutors should constitute the basis of the pastoral network, yet the time-table frequently makes it impossible for them to take any responsibility for guidance, for example, because they see their tutor groups for only ten minutes each day for registration purposes (Galloway, 1985a). Another organisational issue which is often overlooked is provision of time for meetings of the team of tutors.

The pastoral team operates at two levels. The heads of year form one level, usually coordinated by a deputy head. This team will plan the overall guidance programme, deciding which areas should be covered within the curriculum of individual subjects and which should be included in the tutorial programme. The second level consists of each head of year with his or her team of form tutors. The tutorial programme produced by the heads of year will not contain a detailed plan for each month's work. This is a matter for discussion within each of the tutorial teams, coordinated by the head of year.

Heads of year are not only responsible for detailed planning of the tutorial programme with their team of tutors. They are also responsible for ensuring that form tutors are alert to the special educational needs of pupils within their respective tutor groups. This is an important aspect of pastoral care, but to see how it can operate most effectively we must first consider some wider policy issues raised by pupils with special educational needs.

## SPECIAL EDUCATIONAL NEEDS: SOME IMPLICATIONS FOR ADMINISTRATORS

### Prevalence

The conclusion that up to 20 per cent of children will have special educational needs at some stage in their school career (DES, 1978) is not, contrary to popular belief, dependent on recent research. Indeed, the same conclusion could have been reached on perfectly adequate research data at any time in the last fifty years (Galloway and Goodwin, 1986). The Warnock Report's 'evidence' was based on a statistical artefact and a political compromise. The statistical artefact results from the way behaviour-screening instruments and tests of intelligence or educational attainment are produced. This ensures they identify low-achieving, dull, or difficult pupils. The number of children identified depends purely on the preferred cut-off point. Warnock's committee could perfectly well have argued that 5, 10 or even 30 per cent of children had special educational needs, and still have drawn on research evidence to support their case. Yet in saying that pupils had special needs they were making a political as well as an educational judgement, by implying that ordinary teachers should not be expected to cater for these children without extra support or extra training. It is in this sense that the figure of 20 per cent represents a political compromise.

## Responses at national level

In any system of free and compulsory education the government has to decide how to cater for pupils who cannot easily be taught effectively in ordinary classes. The first decision, though, concerns the proportion of children considered to need such help. In Britain the government's reaction to the Warnock Report was to pass the 1981 Education Act. This accepted Warnock's criteria for defining special needs, but gave LEAs no additional resources to cater for them. Moreover, the government made clear that formal assessment was only essential for the 2 per cent of children who had traditionally been placed in designated special schools or classes. It thus sought to by-pass, if not altogether ignore, the 20 per cent recommendation.

Having decided what proportion of children should receive 'special' attention, and by implication special resources, the government has to decide how to cater for these children. Children with severe intellectual disability obviously require specialised teaching, though whether this should take place in a unit based in an ordinary school or in a special school is controversial. Children with sensory disabilities also require specialised teaching. With resources this can be provided in ordinary classes and, at least in Britain, Swann (1985) shows that special school placement is becoming less frequent. In the same article Swann also shows that children with moderate learning difficulties and adjustment difficulties (formerly known as ESN(M) and maladjusted) are now more likely to be placed in designated special schools or classes than before publication of the Warnock Report. This is particularly ironic in view of the international evidence that children with moderate learning difficulties make better educational progress in ordinary than in special classes, and the lack of evidence that the personal and social adjustment of children with adjustment difficulties is helped by special classes (Galloway and Goodwin, 1986).

Yet this does not imply that government, or in Britain LEAs, can adopt a wholesale policy of integration into the mainstream for these children. As Tomlinson (1982) has argued, special schools and classes can be seen as a response to pressure from teachers to remove problem children from ordinary classes. In order to maintain teachers' morale and to ensure that other pupils do not suffer from attention given to those with special needs, if for no other reasons, a policy of integration requires attention to resources in ordinary schools.

## Responses at school level

A popular response to problems of disruptive behaviour is to establish special units or classes for the pupils concerned. These classes are usually staffed from the school's regular resources, without special help from the LEA. They are seen as a way of enabling ordinary teaching to continue undisturbed, while at the same time preparing the pupils for return to ordinary classes. Unfortunately, the evidence suggests that the second objective is not always achieved. Nor is there any evidence that they are successful in reducing the perceived need to suspend disruptive pupils from attendance. On the other hand, there is clear evidence that factors within the school do exert an important influence on pupils' behaviour (Galloway et al., 1982). The evidence suggests that disruptive behaviour reflects tensions in a school's organisation and curriculum and these are not solved by establishing special units.

The same applies to provision for children with learning difficulties. Some schools still place these children in a separate class in spite of evidence that this does little to promote their educational progress. Others withdraw selected pupils for additional help in particular subjects. This usually results in short term gains but these are often lost on return to the mainstream (Tobin and Pumfrey, 1976). The implication is either that extra help should be provided on a long-term basis, or that the curriculum in the withdrawal class should be more closely based on that of the ordinary class than is usually the case.

The wide variations between schools in their pupils' behaviour, and to a lesser extent in their educational progress, cannot be attributed solely to catchment factors (Rutter et al., 1979). Elsewhere I have reviewed evidence that many pupils with special educational needs can be seen as the product of a social climate and curriculum in their schools (Galloway, 1985a). It follows that special or remedial classes are based on the false premise that the problem lies primarily with the children. This has some interesting implications.

## Curriculum implications

Hargreaves (1983) draws attention to the low esteem in which low ability pupils in comprehensive schools hold the special curricula designed for them. He argues that these curricula transmit a socially divisive message to all pupils in the school. This sociological perspective should be seen in the light of empirical evidence that children with special needs seldom benefit educationally from separate special provision in an ordinary school, let alone from transfer to a special school.

The challenge, then, is to find ways to adapt the mainstream curriculum to cater successfully for special educational needs. That, however, is only feasible if subject teachers in the mainstream feel they have adequate support to cater for these pupils. It implies that each subject department in a secondary school should have immediate access to resources suitable for children with special needs. This is implicitly critical of the popular model of a centralised resource centre based in the special needs department. It also implies that members of this department will work with subject teachers in producing suitable materials, and that they will work with individual pupils in their ordinary classes, in partnership with the regular class teacher, rather than withdraw them for separate teaching. A school in New Zealand which has gone a long way to implement this kind of 'whole school' approach to special educational needs is described elsewhere (Galloway, 1985b).

## ROLE OF GUIDANCE NETWORK AND GUIDANCE CURRICULUM

Two of the tutors' principal guidance responsibilities are to monitor their pupils' progress across the curriculum and to be aware of circumstances that might affect a pupil's progress or social adjustment at school. They will be expected to take a particular interest in pupils known to have special needs. Their responsibility goes further than this. By monitoring pupils' progress across the curriculum and by knowing their pupils as individuals better than other teachers, they also have a responsibility for identifying special needs at an early stage. Particular difficulty in one subject may be attributed by the subject teacher to straightforward lack of ability. The tutor, though, with a wider perspective may recognise that further investigation is needed. Similarly, gradual deterioration in school work may go unspotted by individual teachers, as may difficulties in completing homework due to family circumstances.

It is unreasonable to expect all teachers to be sensitive to the personal or educational difficulties of all pupils. The role of the head of year is to give tutors the guidance and informal in-service training that will enable them to carry out their pastoral responsibilities effectively. At the very least, tutors should recognise the limits to their own competence. In other words, they should know when to seek further advice from the head of year as leader of the tutorial team. For his part, the head of year should know when to seek specialist help, for example from a school counsellor, educational psychologist or school doctor.

## Pastoral curriculum and tutorial programme

A central aim of the pastoral curriculum is to ensure optimum conditions for pupils' progress across the curriculum. Pupils with special needs are clearly likely to require attention in several areas. At the basic level of finding their way around the school or seeking advice about particular problems, for example, they will need more guidance through the induction programme than other children. Later, when the questions of subject choice and careers education arise, they are also likely to need additional attention.

An aim of personal and social education which has attracted relatively little discussion is to contribute to a climate throughout the school which accepts and respects individual differences. It has almost become a cliche that people with disabilities regard their greatest handicap as other people's attitudes. A task for the guidance programme is to develop in pupils a constructive awareness of disability and an attitude which recognises disabled people's right of access to resources in the school and in the community.

## SUMMARY AND CONCLUSIONS

This chapter has described one model for a pastoral network in secondary schools, and has argued that a pastoral curriculum is needed if this network is to operate effectively. Management implications at national and school level have been discussed, with particular reference to the responsibilities of personnel in the pastoral team and the need for in-service training. Responses to pupils with special educational needs have been discussed, with particular reference to the implications of a policy to educate these children in ordinary schools. In this connection it is argued that the pastoral team has an important part to play.

Pastoral care and special educational needs are both topical and controversial issues, at least in Britain. At a time of general contraction in education both are expanding. Experience in Britain and other Western countries suggests that current practices, both in pastoral care and in special educational needs, have led up a number of blind alleys. The challenge for the future is to develop more constructive policies and practices.

## REFERENCES

Baldwin, J. and Wells, H. (1981) Active Tutorial Work, Books 1-5, Oxford: Basil Blackwell.

Button, L. (1981) Group Tutoring for the Form Teacher: Book 1 Lower Secondary School; Book 2 Upper Secondary School, London: Hodder and Stoughton.

Department of Education and Science (DES) (1978) Special Educational Needs (Warnock Report), London: HMSO.

Galloway, D. (1985a) Schools, Pupils and Special Educational Needs, London: Croom Helm.

——— (1985b) 'Meeting special educational needs in the ordinary school, or creating them?, Maladjustment and Therapeutic Education, 3, pp.3-10.

Galloway, D., Bull, C., Blomfield, D. and Seyd, R. (1982) Schools and Disruptive Pupils, London: Longman.

Galloway, D. and Goodwin, C. (1986) The Educating of Disturbing Children: Pupils with Learning and Adjustment Difficulties, London: Longman.

Hargreaves, D.H. (1983) The Challenge of the Comprehensive School: Culture, Curriculum, Community, London:

Routledge & Kegan Paul.

Inner London Education Authority (1984) Improving Secondary Schools (The Hargreaves Report), London: ILEA.

Levitt, E.E. (1963) 'Psychotherapy with children: a further evaluation', Behaviour Research and Therapy, 1, pp. 45-51.

Marland, M. (1980) 'The pastoral curriculum', in Best, R., Jarvis, C. and Ribbins, P. (eds) Perspective in Pastoral Care, London: Heinemann.

——— (1983) 'Preparing for promotion in pastoral care', in Pastoral Care in Education, 1, pp. 24-36.

Mitchell, S. and Rosa, P. (1981) 'Boyhood behaviour problems as precursors of criminality: a fifteen year follow up', Journal of Child Psychology and Psychiatry, 22, pp. 19-23.

Murgatroyd, S. (1983) 'Counselling at a time of change and development', British Psychological Society Education Section Review, 7, pp. 5-9.

Robbins, L.N. (1972) 'Follow up studies of behaviour disorders in children', in Quay, H.C. and Werry, J.S. (eds) Psychopathological Disorders of Childhood, New York: Wiley.

Rutter, M., Maugham, B., Mortimore, P., Ouston, J. and Smith A. (1979) Fifteen Thousand Hours, London: Open Books.

Swann, W. (1985) 'Is the integration of children with special needs happening? An analysis of recent statistics of pupils in special schools', Oxford Review of Education, 11, pp. 3-18.

Tobin, D. and Pumfrey, P. (1976) 'Some long-term effects of the remedial teaching of reading', Educational Review, 29, pp. 1-12.

Tomlinson, S. (1982) The Sociology of Special Education, London: Routledge & Kegan Paul.

# PART 2: INTEGRATION AND LEARNING

# 5 INTEGRATING CHILDREN WITH PHYSICAL IMPAIRMENTS: THE ORMEROD EXPERIENCE

Tim Southgate

Ormerod School is a day special school for children with physical disabilities. In recent years, the school has taken an active approach towards integration and, since 1980, more than a hundred children have moved out into ordinary schools. Aged between four and fifteen, these were children with a very wide range of physical, sensory and learning difficulties.

About half the children have been integrated into their local school or nursery, often with the support of a full- or part-time welfare assistant. The Ormerod staff have usually initiated and coordinated these moves. Visits are made with the child to the prospective school and discussions held regarding any special adaptations and equipment that may appear necessary. The receiving teacher may visit Ormerod School to see the child and discuss his or her management there and, when the move is made, Ormerod staff have usually been available to provide follow-up support.

For those children who, because of physical or other reasons, are not able to be integrated into their local schools, three 'outposts' have been established within mainstream schools and staffed by Ormerod School. The first of these outposts was set up at Marlborough School, a comprehensive school at Woodstock, in 1981. This school was approached because the great majority of its teaching areas are at ground level. The original nine children transferred to Marlborough included two who were cerebral palsied, two with spina bifida and two boys with muscular dystrophy. There were also two boys who were said to be 'delicate'. With them went a teacher (in fact, two half teachers) and a welfare assistant. Another boy who, instead of going to Marlborough with his classmates, had been integrated into his local school but who was experiencing difficulties, joined them after a term and a steady stream of children have followed the same path ever since.

All the children at Marlborough between eleven and sixteen have traditionally been taught in mixed-ability classes and at that time it was the headteachers' expectation that, if children needed additional support, this should be provided in the ordinary classroom. No special class, department or unit was established therefore because such an arrangement was unacceptable to the headteacher of the receiving school. A separately identifiable support system would have conflicted with the headteacher's mixed-ability, non-labelling stance and, instead the children from Ormerod were fully integrated into ordinary classes according to their age. They were retained on the roll of the special school which was thus able to provide the staffing necessary to support them within the classroom.

Over a period of six years, about thirty Ormerod children have attended Marlborough and generally with considerable success. These children have been immersed in a much richer social and learning environment than could have been provided by a small special school and between them they obtained fifty passes in CSE. This success owes as much to the particular philosophy and organisation of the host school and to the flexibility and skill of its teaching staff as to the support provided by the special school.

Two children did not share in this success. Both experienced considerable difficulty in maintaining the level of reading and information handling required of a pupil in a mainstream secondary school. As time went on the differentials between their attainments and those around them widened considerably and, as a result, both began to present behavioural difficulties which eventually precipitated their removal. Had it been possible for these children to be withdrawn for part of the time in order to meet their special learning needs, it is possible that they could have been maintained within the Marlborough situation. However, because such a withdrawal approach was not an option, these and other Ormerod children of secondary age were unable to gain the undoubted benefits of integration.

When the Marlborough outpost was established, the spectrum of needs among the children at Ormerod School was very wide. Although most had physical disabilities, these varied from quite mild to severe and complex. Others were able-bodied but had health problems. Many children were within the average ability range but some were very able while others had quite severe learning difficulties. It was the difficulties encountered in trying to meet this variety of special needs that provided much of the incentive to set up the Marlborough secondary integration scheme. The younger children at Ormerod at that time presented a similarly wide range of physical and curricular needs and so, in 1982, an integration arrangement for children aged between five and nine years was established with the cooperation of the headteacher of Bernwood First School.

Fearing that these much younger children would be more vulnerable than their secondary counterparts, a special room was allocated and equipped. A nearby toilet was also modified to provide an accessible changing area. These enhanced facilities were devised and financed by Ormerod School and were intended to provide a base for the children from which they could venture forth for selected doses of 'integration'. An initial group of eight children was selected and a teacher and classroom assistant from Ormerod allocated to support them. However, within a few weeks, it was clear that the children and staff felt more isolated in their 'special' room than they had in their special school. Several alternative arrangements were tried. Eventually a structure similar to that at Marlborough emerged with the children fully integrated into the ordinary classrooms according to their ages and supported there by the staff from Ormerod. Again, the children experienced considerable benefits from their mainstream experience. In particular, they demonstrated gains in their social skills, becoming increasingly confident and outgoing. Gradually, most of these children moved on either to their local primary schools or, at the age of nine, with their classmates into middle school.

In 1985, as the remnants of the first group of children were about to leave Bernwood, a second group replaced them. Clearly, we had failed to learn any lessons from the earlier arrangement because, again fearful for the children's safety, a considerable amount of money was spent creating a new special needs base area, much larger and more attractive than before. Before many weeks were out, however, the children were again spending almost all their time in the ordinary classrooms. A new system was devised which not only enabled the Ormerod pupils to be integrated but enhanced the educational situation for the Bernwood children as well. Two of the Bernwood classes were combined and the children divided into three new groups. The two Bernwood teachers took one group each and the Ormerod teacher became the class teacher for the third group. Each group comprised about eighteen children which made it much easier to accommodate the physically disabled children and their additional equipment. As well as wheelchairs and walking aids, two of the children had their own computer systems as writing aids. The Ormerod classroom assistant spent part of her time working with a younger boy who was in a separate group and a second teacher from Ormerod School provided additional individual teaching for some of the children, in particular Joe whose case is outlined below. Speech and physiotherapy were also provided on site.

Next door to Ormerod is Bayswater Middle School. This school occupies a large building with several flights of steps and stairs and, while much of it would be inaccessible to a child in a wheelchair, it is suitable for those who are ambulant. Its proximity to Ormerod makes it an appropriate setting for children who are mobile but who need some additional part-time support. Two of the children who were vacating places at Bernwood in 1985 were to transfer to Bayswater School. Both were mobile, one being cerebral palsied and the other having cystic fibrosis. At the same time, three children who had remained at Ormerod emerged as candidates for integration. These three were 'delicate' children being mobile but having both medical and learning problems. The headteacher of Bayswater School agreed that these five children could all attend his school and an Ormerod teacher was allocated to the task of supporting them. It was felt that any welfare assistance could be provided as and when required by staff from Ormerod.

As the plans for this middle-school arrangement developed, Peter, a hearing-impaired child, was also included and his case is described in more detail below. The six children, all between nine and eleven years old, moved to Bayswater and were placed in classes according to age. One, Vicky, had only recently returned to Ormerod following an unsuccessful period in another middle school. She was placed in the same class as Gemma, her best friend from Ormerod and, when an initial period of emotional difficulty for both of them had been overcome, they settled in and their integration continues successfully. Two of the boys, Peter and David, were provided with computers as writing aids in the classroom. A further computer was installed in a small room allocated to the Ormerod support teachers for individual work. One boy, Paul, needed a great deal of support. His very considerable learning disabilities became increasingly apparent at Bayswater. Eventually, he was receiving individual support within or outside the classroom for the greater part of the week and still was unable to cope with the curricular demands being made upon him. At the end of the year, it was agreed that he should be withdrawn and he transferred to a residential school for children with learning difficulties.

The remaining child at Bayswater, Graham, had never actually attended the Ormerod building. At his local first school he was finding life difficult because of his cystic fibrosis. He was admitted to the school roll in 1982 and immediately joined those children moving to the Bernwood outpost. He was maintained there through the efforts of the Ormerod teacher, the classroom assistant and the staff of the receiving school and moved on to Bayswater when that scheme commenced in September, 1985. Graham required tipping at school three times every day in order to clear his lungs and a rota of classroom assistants was organised for this purpose. However, the resulting succession of faces proved very disconcerting to Graham himself and, instead, a welfare assistant was taken on and trained specifically for this work and paid out of the Ormerod School funds. Eventually, however, Graham's health deteriorated and he died after attending his middle school for two terms.

It is often remarked that 'there will always be some children who cannot be integrated'. The speaker may mean to imply or the listener may infer that the needs of certain children, because they have disabilities which are particularly severe or complex, simply cannot be met within an ordinary school. However, the reality is less simple and the degree of success of a child's integration is by no means proportional to the extent of physical handicap or indeed to intelligence. The case histories below are included to demonstrate that children with disabilities of great severity and complexity can receive their education within ordinary schools while children whose problems by comparison appear superficially to be minor fail.

## PETER

Peter is profoundly deaf and his physical impairment makes writing tiring and untidy. He attended Ormerod School since the age of four, receiving a great deal of individual teaching. Peter is a bright boy and, through the Paget Gorman signing system, his language and literacy gradually developed. A computer system and a special word processor program enabled him to write and motivated him to increase greatly his written output. His progress was such that, as he approached secondary age, it became necessary to reconsider his educational placement. Peter required a broader curriculum than could be provided at secondary level in a small special school and, because of his hearing impairment, he would need to develop alternative methods of communication and particularly his literacy skills.

Peter's deafness had become his greater special need and the alternative to a special school for physically handicapped children seemed to be a residential school for the deaf. This was the course advocated by the authority's support services but it was not one which appealed to Peter or to his parents. They were adamant that he should remain at home as part of the family and, anyway, the residential schools investigated presented various problems. Those that employed signing used British Sign Language and, while it will probably be desirable for Peter to learn this system at some stage so that he can communicate readily within the deaf community, this was a challenge neither he nor his parents were yet ready to face. In addition, the schools for the deaf are not generally geared to the needs of physically handicapped children. One, for instance, arranged some integration for its pupils. However, this was only in the practical subjects in which Peter would be at a disadvantage and the children had to reach the comprehensive school concerned on their bicycles.

## The Ormerod experience

Within the authority, there was no secondary day provision for children with profound hearing loss. In order for him to remain at home, therefore, it was necessary to devise an integration scheme specifically for him. Through their work with Peter and other children with speech and language handicaps, several members of the Ormerod staff had acquired fluency in Paget Gorman Signed Speech. Alongside Ormerod School is Bayswater Middle School and this offered a mainstream curriculum appropriate to Peter's needs. It was therefore proposed that Peter should remain on the Ormerod roll but attend Bayswater School with support from the Ormerod staff. A classroom assistant agreed to take on the role of signing interpreter. Peter would also need to spend part of each week with a specialist language teacher who was fluent in Paget Gorman signing in order to help maintain his language at the level necessary to cope with the increasing demands of the curriculum. One of the Ormerod teachers agreed to take on this task.

Peter and his parents approved of this proposed arrangement and the Chief Education Officer agreed to the funding necessary to make it a reality. In September 1985, Peter moved to Bayswater School and was provided with a signing interpreter for fifteen hours each week and was withdrawn for extra language work for 0.3 of each week. The intention was that, for the remainder of the week, he should be unsupported and thus have to develop his own alternative communication strategies. In the event, Peter's proposed move sparked off an arrangement whereby a further five children on the Ormerod roll were integrated into Bayswater School. Two of these had been integrated into Bernwood School and were now nine years old. The other three were children with medical conditions who were still attending Ormerod. These five, like Peter, were placed in ordinary classes and an Ormerod teacher was assigned full-time to Bayswater School to support them. As a fluent signer, she was also able to provide additional support for Peter: for instance, during morning assembly.

Peter's integration at Bayswater has been a considerable success. This has been due not only to the support provided for him by the Ormerod staff but also to the professional commitment of the teachers at Bayswater who have extended their high expectations of children to include Peter. Equally important to this success, however, has been Peter himself. His positive personality and enthusiasm have made him many friends in spite of his communication problems and, in his recent school report, he was described by his teacher as 'an asset to the class'.

## JOE

Joe is registered blind and is severely physically handicapped. He joined the infant class at Ormerod School when he was five. Like Peter, Joe received a great deal of individual teaching. He was included in a computer development project at the school with the aim particularly of helping him to develop his language and literacy skills. Although he had some vision, he could not see well enough to read even quite large letters. He was therefore introduced to rebuses, symbols that represent words, and speech synthesis was used so that when he pressed the symbols on a special keyboard the computer would speak the appropriate word. In this way Joe learnt to build sentences and by means of colour-coding, he learnt his way around the ordinary computer keyboard. A special word processor program incorporating speech synthesis helped him to begin to write his own words and to learn to spell.

When, in 1985, a second group of children from Ormerod was integrated into Bernwood, it was felt that Joe's skills had developed sufficiently to be able to go with them. Like Peter, his friendly personality has enabled him to build relationships with other children and adults and he has thrived in the wider world of the mainstream school. As described above, Joe was placed in one of three small classes made possible by the additional teaching resources provided by Ormerod School. He also received regular extra teaching from a second Ormerod teacher and, by working on the computer with its speech synthesiser, learnt to spell a long list of words which he was eventually able to combine into sentences and so create his own written passages. Joe has remained at his first school beyond the normal age range in order to allow him time to build these skills but he will shortly be eleven and will then transfer to Marlborough School.

## JOHN AND SARAH

Those working in mainstream schools usually have little difficulty in recognising that children who are physically handicapped may have some sort of special needs. In this respect, those whose needs are not so visible may be at a considerable disadvantage. When the first Ormerod children arrived at Marlborough in September 1981, it was immediately clear to those watching them disembark that six or seven of them had mobility and communication problems. John, in his Marlborough uniform, was less noticeable. No outward signs indicated that he had a serious blood condition and he rapidly disappeared into the crowd. However, John's condition had caused him to miss most of his early schooling and, as a result, he had developed severe reading difficulties. As those around him progressed, John, despite considerable help in the classroom, was left further and further behind. Uncomprehending, his boredom led him into fights and bruises which eventually led his father to withdraw him from the school. He transferred to a comprehensive school nearer his home where there was a special needs withdrawal unit and in this situation he was able to receive the help he needed and to make progress.

Sarah was also not physically disabled but she too had learning and behaviour difficulties and needs that could not be met within the ordinary classroom. Eventually, Sarah's parents felt that she could not continue at Marlborough. However, a return to Ormerod, where the remaining children were now considerably more physically handicapped than those who were there during her earlier attendance, also seemed inappropriate. No suitable provision was available and she continues to receive individual tuition at home. Like Paul at Bayswater, both John and Sarah were among those children for whom total integration in a mainstream classroom is not appropriate and who may, without provision suited to their needs, react against integration altogether.

## MARLBOROUGH: THE NEXT STEP

As more Ormerod children of secondary age have been integrated, the group remaining behind has diminished in size and has increasingly comprised those children for whom, like John, Sarah and Paul, the 'total' integration offered at Marlborough is inappropriate. However, as this group has diminished so has the quality of their learning environment. When, in 1987, it seemed that the number of secondary children remaining in the Ormerod building in the near future would probably be in single figures, it was decided to take steps to move them all on to a mainstream site.

The new headteacher at Marlborough agreed to set aside a large classroom for the use of the children from Ormerod and a physiotherapy area and new special toilets were built. From this base, the children will be integrated into the ordinary classes as and when appropriate. Some children will spend all their time in ordinary classes, only returning to the base area to use the special toilets or for physiotherapy. Others might spend almost all of their time in the base room, only joining in with the ordinary classes for certain activities. The advantage of having this base within Marlborough is that the amount and nature of integration may be adjusted to suit each individual child. Within the base area, children will work on individual programmes with objectives dependent upon the nature of their disabilities and needs.

It might seem that to provide a special base room is only to make the same assumptions and to repeat the same mistakes that were made at Bernwood on two occasions. It would be nice to think that this special provision will eventually be similarly redundant. However, the circumstances in a comprehensive school are quite different from those in a first school. Children are faced with much greater demands both academically and emotionally. They must handle much more information and responsibility at an age when they are facing other great changes in their lives. It therefore seems likely that this special provision will continue to be necessary for some children, allowing us to meet their special educational needs and allowing them to gain some of the benefits of integration. Within one building, it will be possible to offer the whole continuum of special needs provision from total integration without support to total segregation (although hopefully not too much of the latter). If successful, it will no longer be necessary for children of secondary age with physical disabilities to be educated away from their able-bodied peers. The segregation of these children in special schools will be ended.

# 6 INTEGRATING PUPILS WITH BEHAVIOURAL DIFFICULTIES INTO MAINSTREAM SCHOOLS

Jackie Sunderland

## INTRODUCTION

For many years central government documents have suggested that the principle of integration was official government policy. In 1954, Circular 276 stated that 'no handicapped child should be sent to a special school who can satisfactorily be educated in an ordinary school. Yet, through the 1970s, special education provision in segregated schools for almost all categories of handicap increased. Furthermore, when the overall growth in special education provision had ceased, Swann (1985) showed that in the case of pupils with learning difficulties and the maladjusted, there was clear evidence of a trend towards increasing segregation.

In the Warnock Report (1978) there was evidence to show limited integration taking place nationally of pupils with physical and sensory disability. Schemes involving the maladjusted appear to be the result of local rather than national initiatives. With the passing of the 1981 Education Act, the principle that pupils with special needs should be educated in ordinary schools became part of education law. In the absence of specific central policy towards that end, this is an opportunity to look at a local initiative to point directions which might be pursued within the general framework of the 1981 Act.

Northern House Special School, in Oxford, has pursued a policy of integrating into ordinary schools pupils with behavioural difficulties. This chapter will summarise the background and main issues in this policy and how the integration programme originated and evolved to its present form. In a field such as this it is not possible to produce 'case-studies' that draw attention to essential strategies for integration because each programme is tailored to the needs of the individual pupils integrating in a specific school. It is hoped, however, that this account will encourage others who are anticipating the problems of integrating pupils with behaviour problems, and that a high degree of success is possible.

## GENERAL BACKGROUND AND MAIN ISSUES

Hegarty (1982) has maintained that among the variety of reasons why pupils are placed in special schools is that ordinary schools have failed them, and will continue to fail them, unless considerable changes are made in the ordinary sector. Tomlinson (1982) sees the growth of the special education sector as a political response to a crucial dilemma affecting the education system, namely the question of what preparation for the future should be offered a group of pupils who are unwilling or unable to participate in the system as we know it and in the future may well be unemployed. She says that the teaching profession has complied with the expansion of the special needs sector because mainstream teachers have an interest in avoiding dealing with special needs pupils and that special education teachers need referrals in order to remain in business. As Swann has indicated, rather than the 1981 Act resulting in a reduction of special provision, the reverse has been the case. This is possibly because, in some LEAs, the Act has led to changes in practice in the identification and assessment of pupils, and there are therefore more identified needs.

Booth (1983) supports Tomlinson's thesis with figures to show that, in the fifteen years from 1961 to 1976, there was a 273 per cent increase in pupils labelled maladjusted. Although the picture across the country is obviously varied and in some LEAs statementing may be avoided because of the legal consequences, overall there has been a higher rate of referrals for special education than hitherto.

Many special needs pupils, once they are out of the system, are no longer a problem as long as they can find work. Pupils with special educational needs, especially those presenting behavioural problems, are sometimes only at odds with the school system. The special need condition is perhaps simply a result of the interaction between pupil and school rather than some inbuilt disability on the part of the pupil. Perhaps it is school policies we need to examine as well as pupil needs.

## Pupils and teachers in mainstream schools

We need to consider the process of integration in relation to special schools, and what happens when a pupil is integrated back into ordinary education, and equally to consider the nature of the process when a pupil is segregated from ordinary schools in the first place. In the two situations the attitudes and behaviour of pupils and teachers are crucial as pupils move from one type of school to the other. Are teacher attitudes more flexible and supportive of pupils with behavioural difficulties in the integrated situation? Can it be said, at the point of referral when options open to teachers often seem more restricted, that this is the reason why the removal of a pupil is seen as the only solution? The classification of pupils as having special needs is a process which is not independent of the nature of mainstream schools. We need to be aware of the practices in ordinary schools that lead to segregation if we are to follow a policy of returning pupils to a system in which they have already failed.

## Referred pupils

Pupils in Northern House School have all experienced a breakdown in personal relationships leading to exclusion or plans to exclude. Pupils are referred at the age of seven to eight years so that few have not experienced ordinary schooling. The school has sixty-two pupils on roll from various parts of Oxfordshire, all of whom have been referred to the School Psychological Service, and statemented. Before arriving at Northern House attempts will have been made to cater for their needs in a variety of ways through extra teaching, welfare assistance, programmes developed by educational psychologists, attendance at special units, and the involvement of other agencies such as hospital paediatric departments and Child Guidance.

The younger pupils at Northern House School are usually more disturbed than their older peers. A possible reason for this is that primary teachers are often reluctant to admit that their pupils cannot be managed and those referred are the exceptionally difficult pupils. It is unfortunate that many teachers are reluctant to admit what they perceive to be failure because, as a result, the disturbed pupils may remain in a situation where they not only cause acute distress to others but continue to damage themselves. In addition to problems associated with teachers' reluctance to admit failure, however, children may often have very difficult behaviour patterns and true disturbance and some of the older pupils would have benefited considerably had they arrived sooner.

## THE PUPILS AT NORTHERN HOUSE

To describe the pupils at Northern House School as emotionally disturbed is not an appropriate generalisation: they are maladjusted. This definition covers a wide range since it simply means that the pupil is not adjusted to one or any number of various situations and/or people. These may include school, parents, home environment, siblings, peers, class teachers, class and certain relations. Maladjustment to any of these may cause a pattern of behaviour which cannot be managed in school, and often cannot be managed at home.

Some schools refer more pupils out to special schools than others, either because the school has a large population of maladjusted pupils or because its tolerance of and skills for dealing with maladjusted pupils are low. These differences cannot fully be attributed to differences in pupil characteristics (Galloway, 1980). The likelihood of being referred depends at least as much on the particular school attended as on any constitutional factors affecting behaviour, or even the actual behaviour presented. Rutter et al. (1979) point out that through the experiences they provide, schools affect the attainment and behaviour of their pupils. Children in mainstream said to have special needs are partly a product of the policies and practices of their school. Tolerance and skill in a particular school may be low because of a lack of resources or the means to develop such skills. Adequate resources are, however, not generally available in mainstream schools and not many LEAs are farsighted enough to have a policy for prevention rather than segregation.

## The school

Northern House has approximately twenty pupils in the lower school and forty in the upper school. Although in the lower school the pupils are aged up to ten years, the curriculum is infant school orientated, and for some pupils it offers a preschool type of experience. The upper school is organised as an upper junior-middle school with exchanges of teachers for specialist subjects. One of the classes is exceptionally large and has seventeen pupils, all of them either integrating into mainstream on a part-time basis or being prepared for integration. As a result, although on the class register there are seventeen pupils, the class is usually considerably smaller.

## Northern House and integration

When Northern House had four classes and pupils had to leave at the age of eleven years, usually about half of the leavers went to out-county boarding schools and the other half went into mainstream. There was no programme of integration and pupils were simply put into mainstream schools on the premise that they were less likely to need out-county boarding than the others in their year group who had to leave. Many of the pupils so placed quickly failed to cope and were sent out of the county at a later date after another traumatic encounter with mainstream education. Although teachers from Northern House occasionally visited the mainstreamed pupils this activity was spasmodic and could not be seen as presenting a service to the pupils, because all staff had a full teaching commitment and no free time.

In 1979, with the arrival of a new headteacher, two pupils were felt not to need special schooling because their behaviour and social interaction with pupils and adults were thought appropriate for mainstream. Because it was considered important that the pupils should be educated in their local community rather than in the middle school near to Northern House, visits were made to their neighbourhood schools with a view to gradual integration. This needed to be gradual since both pupils had attended Northern House for more than three years and neither had experience of mainstream schooling within recent memory. The two schools were approached and briefed in detail about the pupils in terms of successes, weaknesses and problems, and both agreed to take these local pupils on a part-time basis with regular support from Northern House School.

Initially, the pupils attended their schools on a one-day-a-week basis on days when they would have subjects in which they would be likely to succeed. In preliminary discussions, as well as making valuable links with the pupils' teachers, it was possible to gain knowledge of what a mainstream school expected and required of a child and also what kind of child could be successful and maintain him or herself in that particular school. From the outset it was apparent that schools varied greatly in their expectations of pupils and it was essential that any future integration should take this into account and take great care to match a child with a school which would cater for her or his needs. At this time the supporting teacher from Northern House was the headteacher since any other member of staff would need to be freed from the normal teaching commitment. In this instance the support consisted of liaising with the headteacher and staff in the mainstream school and arranging several meetings with the pupils' parents. In addition, the pupils in the receiving class were briefed and prepared for the integration so that, when the pupil arrived, the process proceeded smoothly.

At the beginning of the integration scheme, when Oxford City changed from a two- to a three-tier system of schooling, the upper age limit for pupils at Northern House School was eleven years. Since Northern House was surrounded by middle schools, the integration of pupils was severely impeded. In 1981, the school expanded its age range and the school increased from thirty-eight to fifty pupils. Out-county boarding was costing, at that time, around £10,000 per child per year, and it was decided that the money should be spent on developing expertise in Oxfordshire. The savings from this policy change meant that extra resourcing could be directed towards expanding facilities at Northern House School in the provision of an art room and gymnasium and in developing a more appropriate curriculum for pupils of middle school age. This allowed the integration programme to expand further.

The principal aim was not to integrate pupils so much as to achieve a teaching environment appropriate to the needs of the pupils. Success in this area would then lead to integration as a by-product. Not all schools have integration as an eventual aim, possibly because they believe that when the pupils become adjusted, their adjustment is in fact school-specific.

In my opinion, the general aim for all pupils with any category of disability should be eventual integration if at all possible, always bearing in mind the well-being of the pupil concerned. As can be seen from the development of the integration policy at Northern House, the process, which should be tailored to individual needs, must be very carefully planned and be an integral part of the general ethos of the school. For many special schools, the general aim seems to be to facilitate the adjustment of the pupil to a particular school. At Northern House this is obviously extremely important but it is not an end in itself.

Becoming adjusted to a special school can be the first step to becoming adjusted to mainstream school and to society at large. It may be argued that pupils from a special school cannot be expected to integrate successfully into mainstream because it is so different from the school to which they are adjusted. However, the whole point is that they are not only adjusted to the special school.

## The importance of support

In practice, two teachers at Northern House School now share the integration class: one teaches for that part of the week which they spend at Northern House, the other travels to support pupils in their local middle and upper schools. In this way, both teachers not only continue to gain experience in their support-liaison role in mainstream, but they also continue to teach and counsel the pupils in the more familiar surroundings of the special school. Gradually, the pupils spend an increasing amount of time unsupported in ordinary lessons and support continues for varying lengths of time according to the needs of both the pupils integrated and the mainstream staff with whom they come into contact. Pupils who need to talk over any problems know that help is at hand, and mainstream staff who may not have time to follow up an unexplained absence or an unusal lapse in behaviour can refer the matter to the support teacher who, if necessary, will pursue the case to a satisfactory conclusion. This aspect of the support teacher's role is most important since the integrating pupil is very vulnerable and frequently needs to be reassured and encouraged. A single outburst of unruly behaviour or failure to attend school might be an indication of an underlying problem which may have passed unnoticed and minor incidents can quickly escalate into what appears to the pupil as an impossible situation.

Without exception, the pupils seem to have a desire to make their integration succeed, and this in itself puts them under pressure. Early detection of problems and effective trouble-shooting by the support teacher is an essential ingredient towards a successful integration and a well-adjusted pupil. If the support is not available or is withdrawn because of an administrative directive, the months of careful preparation may be wasted and the integration may break down. The effects on the pupil in such a situation can be damaging and, for this reason, the Northern House team continues to support the pupil for as long as is considered desirable and necessary.

## No age bar to integration

Now that pupils may remain at Northern House until the age of thirteen years, integration is not exclusively for pupils at the upper age limit when transfer to another school becomes necessary. There is no age bar for integration: rather there is a flexible approach within the school so that there are pupils in the upper school who may be a year younger than the oldest pupils in the lower school. At present, there is a class in the lower school which can be identified as a potential integration group and out of eight pupils, two will be going back into mainstream at least on a half- to one-day-a-week basis long before they reach the upper school. The age of the pupil is not the important factor.

The lower school scheme is currently developing differently from the process for the older pupils. Rather than each pupil having an individual programme in his or her local mainstream school, the younger pupils as a group attend a local first school. They therefore have the support of their friends and class teacher in the mainstream school and the geographical complications for the support teacher are reduced. At present, the support teacher is a musician and the first school is able to take advantage of this for their own pupils even though there is an increase in class size because of the integration.

Since the integration programme was started, one pupil has been fully integrated within eighteen months of being admitted to the special school. This pupil had developed a pattern of behaviour in mainstream in which he continually failed. When this happens, it does not mean that a pupil is totally inadequate or that his total behaviour is inappropriate. At Northern House School, because of the credit system, teaching methods and small classes, it is possible for the pupil to develop positive and successful responses to adults and academic situations which would not have been possible in mainstream.

Behaviour in mainstream which causes widespread disruption and distress does not have the same effect or cause the same problems in a special school. Sometimes teachers in ordinary schools simply do not have the time to cope with the needs of pupils who disrupt. They sometimes feel that the only option open to them is to exclude the offending pupil. Once in the special school some pupils never present the same behaviour. Pupils with a history of four or five violent temper tantrums in a week may find that after one, in which books and desks are knocked everywhere, such behaviour does not have the same effect. Obviously, some pupils continue to have outbursts, but gradually, they find they do not need to or they do not need to have them so often. When a pupil has built up a good reputation and is able to succeed and make relationships with peers and adults, it is then possible that integration may be considered. However, because in ordinary schools teachers are under pressure with large classes and limited resources, it is important to give them support when pupils are re-integrated.

## Changes to make integration possible

A major change in attitudes is needed in relation to maladjusted behaviour. At the point of referral there is a tendency for the teacher to feel that he or she has failed in the normal task of educating, relationships are strained to breaking point, everyone feels more stressed and negative attitudes ensue. Being labelled maladjusted has a negative effect on the pupil and there is a general feeling that the pupil should not be in an ordinary school. At the point of integration, however, having been officially labelled maladjusted can have a positive effect. The receiving teacher is being asked to take on a pupil who is known to have problems. If there are difficulties with the pupil then they are not unexpected. It is not a sign of the teacher's personal failure, and support will be at hand to help deal with the situation. Because the pupil is known to have been a problem in the past, a teacher taking on somebody else's failure rates a certain amount of esteem, and status may be gained by adopting an open and positive attitude to the integration process. Instead of having to face difficulties alone, the teacher receives support which is not normally available for troublesome pupils in a crisis situation in ordinary schools. Maintaining positive teacher attitudes is crucial to success in integration, and time spent with receiving teachers usually far exceeds the amount of time support staff need to spend in class with the pupil. With positive attitudes by teacher and pupil, integration has a much higher chance of success.

Parental attitudes about special school placements are beginning to change as a result of the new initiatives towards integration. Because pupils no longer spend all of their statutory schooling in a special school, parents can view the period of time spent in a special school more positively. The possibility of integration may help parents to agree to their child being transferred to a special school. In addition, the pupils themselves see many of their peers moving in and out of mainstream schools on a regular basis and therefore have some positive patterns which they can follow themselves. An integration policy enables a special school to exhibit for the pupils a notion of success which is related to 'normal' mainstream schools rather than success solely in relation to the special school. Whilst for some of the pupils this may not be directly relevant, for many the aim towards eventual reintegration is important and motivating. At Northern House School, the integration process is one of the ways in which positive patterns are presented to pupils and these are self-reinforcing.

Success can never be guaranteed when a new group of pupils embarks on a programme of integration. However, since the appointment of the support teacher was made, only one pupil has had to be withdrawn and this was done because of academic rather than behavioural difficulties. Some parents are understandably anxious that their child be integrated into ordinary education but this is not always appropriate or advisable. What is important is that any integration scheme is carried out with thought and planning. Sometimes it is the case that pupil behaviour does not change with any great speed on being admitted to a special school. It takes time for the new regime, its pattern of tolerance, teaching methods, management strategies and philosophy to make an impact. Crucial to all this is the change that is part of attitudes toward the pupil: change that is required both in ordinary as well as special schools.

In dealing with pupils with behaviour problems some teachers are reluctant to take early action or to use the resources that are to hand. Some teachers have had the experience that, when requested, neither the help nor other resources are made available. The fact that positive attitudes can be engendered in mainstream teachers, by having integration support staff working with them, shows that change is possible. This places emphasis on the quality of the work of the support teacher who may have to demonstrate competence, and hence credibility, by effectively teaching groups in both special and ordinary schools.

Every integration programme at Northern House School is tailored to the needs of particular pupils. Not every integration programme works smoothly and some never achieve what might be considered complete success. Although it is not realistic to have a policy of integration at all costs, a general philosophy towards such an objective may often allow more to be achieved than was originally thought possible. The Northern House School experience is a testimony to this.

## REFERENCES

Booth, T., (1983) Eradicating Handicap, Milton Keynes: Open University Press.

Hegarty, S. (1982) 'Integration in the comprehensive school', Educ. Review, 34, pp. 99-105.

Department of Education and Science (1978), Education of Handicapped Children and Young People (Warnock Report), Cmnd 7212, London: HMSO.

Rutter, M., Maugham, B., Mortimore, P., Ouston, J. and Smith A. (1979) Fifteen Thousand Hours, London: Open Books.

Swann, W. (1985) 'Is the integration of children with special needs happening? An analysis of recent statistics of pupils in special schools', Oxford Review of Education, 11 (1), pp. 3-18.

Tomlinson, S. (1982) A Sociology of Special Education, London: Routledge & Kegan Paul.

# 7 INTEGRATION AND SPECIAL EDUCATIONAL NEEDS 14-19

Howard Brayton

## INTRODUCTION

This chapter looks at the question of the education of young people with special educational needs, continuing beyond the statutory leaving age. It is concerned with the location, relevance and effectiveness of provision. Whether the post-sixteen provision is made in school or college, recognition needs to be made of a young person's education up to the age of fourteen years and liaison established with other agencies after the age of nineteen. It argues for a coherent policy statement at both LEA and establishment level; a meaningful curriculum dialogue between establishments, parents and agencies; and a programme of in-service training for teachers and lecturers. In this relatively new area of concern, reference is also made to some agencies and voluntary organisations which are active in the field and to some of their research findings.

## BACKGROUND

In the mid-1970s approximately two-thirds of our sixteen-year-olds left school. Half of them went into unskilled jobs with no training opportunities while the other half became apprentices or took jobs with training. During this time one million unskilled jobs disappeared and the probability is that a further million could do so in the next ten years (Brockington et al., 1985). A consequence of this is that the traditional occupations which many young people with special needs took up no longer exist. The increase in jobs has taken place within the

the service and support industries which require different skills, knowledge and attitudes.

None of this happened suddenly. In 1976 the government introduced pilot schemes of Unified Vocational Preparation (UVP) to help young people leaving school with few or no qualifications. The Holland Report (1977) highlighted the need for courses directed towards helping leavers of low achievement and social competence, and who lacked basic literacy and numeracy skills. Since then the Department of Employment, through the Manpower Services Commission (MSC) has become more and more involved in education and training. The Youth Opportunities Programme (YOP), now the Youth Training Scheme (YTS), was introduced in December 1981, as part of the New Training Initiative (NTI). Recognition of young people with special educational needs is demonstrated in the additional funding available for their training requirements.

There is a growing response to the Technical and Vocational Education Initiative (TVEI) which is open to all young people. Other initiatives include the 17+ Certificate of Pre-Vocational Education (CPVE); the City and Guilds of London Institute Foundation and Vocational Preparation courses; and the 'P' component of the Oxford Certificate of Educational Achievement (OCEA).

Pre-vocational and vocational education, however, must be taken in its widest possible context, as preparation for adult life, and includes social and lifeskills training. For some of our students, the severely and profoundly disabled, work is an unrealistic aim, but the underlying philosophy of educating a student's full potential remains valid. Other students may be well capable of work but unable to hold down a job.

The result of the varying initiatives and funding arrangements has led to entrepreneurial and <u>ad hoc</u> development of provision, not always under the aegis of education services, or in the best interests of young people.

## LEGISLATION

The 1944 Education Act provided for the less severely disabled who were to be educated in ordinary schools. The 1976 Education Act was passed as part of the government's plans to complete the reorganisation of schools along comprehensive lines. Originally the Bill made no reference to pupils with special educational needs until it reached the House of Lords when an amendment brought about Section 10 which would have modified provisions for special needs that existed in the 1944 Education Act. The Lords' amendment was aimed towards an integration policy so that special education was to be provided in ordinary schools except where it 'is impracticable or incompatible with the provision of efficient instruction', or would involve 'unreasonable public expenditure'. In outcome the section was not implemented and its provisions were superseded by the 1981 Education Act. The Warnock Report (1978) drew attention to the fact that:

> local education authorities have a duty, which is not widely recognised, to provide for all young people who want continued full-time education between the ages of sixteen and nineteen, either in school or in an establishment of further education, though not necessarily whichever of the two the individual prefers. (para. 10.28)

The Report recommended 'that where it is in their interests, children with special educational needs should be enabled to stay at school beyond the statutory school leaving age' (para. 10.30). Also, 'that wherever possible, young people with special educational needs should be given the necessary support to enable them to attend courses of further education' (para. 10.39). The Warnock Committee went on to recommend that special vocational courses should be provided in establishments of further education; that there should be special courses of training in social competence and independence; that LEAs should publish their policies and in every establishment of further education designate a member of staff as responsible for the welfare of students with special educational needs. It was also recommended that the progress of a child should be reviewed annually - a proposal that became the Annual Review in the 1981 Education Act, and that pupils with special educational needs should be reassessed at least two years before leaving school - which became the statutory 13+ assessment. This latter assessment should always involve a careers officer.

From the assessment should come a recommendation for post-sixteen options. It may be to remain at school for those who have already embarked upon a recognised course of study; or to transfer to a college of further education with support for a specialised course; or it may entail open or sheltered employment or taking part on a youth training scheme; or it could mean transfer to a training centre for the mentally disabled. Where young people stay at school the curriculum needs to be more than stretching the previous year's leavers' programme for another year or two. A more adult environment needs to be created, allowing more freedom of choice, responsibility and self-advocacy. This is often difficult to achieve when the young adult remains in the same building where she or he has been since the age of eleven - sometimes since primary age.

Possibly more effective is the planned transfer from school to college of further education which begins at fourteen years and incorporates a link or bridging course. Where close cooperation between school and college is developed, students can benefit greatly from a new environment, a more adult approach and new facilities and expertise not available in schools. There is also the opportunity to join vocational courses on a part or full-time basis or to transfer to a YTS programme.

## INTEGRATION

Integration is an emotive word meaning different things to different people and hence needs defining in terms of this chapter. Integration is a process not a state and therefore must be part of a continuum, the opposite extremes of which are: education with peers requiring no additional support, as in the case of a child who may suffer from epilepsy but has never had a fit in school, to the profoundly and severely mentally disabled child who will need specialist one-to-one help. Even in this case 'locational' integration is possible.

There are between these extremes every theoretical possibility: mainstream class with support and aid; mainstream class plus withdrawal; part-time in a special unit or school; or a special school with part-time in mainstream.

In this context integration implies appropriate provision to suit assessed special educational need.

Segregation may be the opposite of integration but as part of the continuum both have a legitimate place. Integration, however, does not just happen. The first requirement is the identification of the special need. Parents have a crucial role as do health visitors in the early years, general practitioners in terms of delayed development and with physical problems, and teachers and lecturers when learning difficulties present themselves.

The second requirement is assessment: the study over time by parents and professionals of the area of difficulty. The Warnock Committee suggested a five-scale structured plan, starting with school staff and leading by stage five to a multi-professional assessment, which may or may not lead to a statement being made and maintained.

The third requirement is a need for records of individual children's progress. On the one hand such records or profiles should set out dates when a parent or professional was involved, or case conference and annual reviews took place and the conclusions arrived at. On the other hand, long- and short-term objectives should be stated and progress noted.

The fourth requirement relates to the attitudes of the staff. Experience has shown that the most successful examples of integration have been those where there has been a total commitment by principals and college staff and a will to make it work. Without this commitment and only a statement of interest by the LEA then every stumbling block will be put in its way and requests for unrealistic levels of resources made.

In 1984 some forty-four young physically disabled students between the ages of 16 and 25 years of age living in Oxfordshire were interviewed to assess their physical, social and educational needs. It is of interest to note the range of comments they made:

- I never got help from the careers service;
- The college do not have a care assistant which I need. I do not like being segregated with disabled people;
- I find it difficult to write fast enough to keep up with lecturers;
- Most disabled people do not want to be treated any differently to anyone else;

- I informed the college that our daughter would be arriving for her interview in a wheelchair. When we arrived we were not given any help to enter the building and we found that the interview was to be held on the first floor;
- All disabled students should be given the same school curriculum as their able-bodied peers and not 'cotton-woolled';
- I am going back over the work I did at school.

These remarks indicate some of the problems the disabled have to face when services are being established. The problems can be listed under access to buildings, help around the building, help in the classroom, attitudes of staff and peers, equal opportunities for all students and a relevant curriculum. Clearly there needs to be a commitment by the LEA both in what it can provide and in discussions with other agencies like Social Services and Health Departments about their roles. Too often the support services available to schools, like educational psychologists, speech therapists, specialist teachers for the visually and hearing impaired, and paramedical services are not available to colleges. Without these, integration is that much harder to accomplish in a satisfactory way.

## CURRICULUM

In Circular 6/81 the attention of LEAs and schools was drawn to the fact that schools should set out in writing the aims which they intended to pursue in relation to the organisation of the curriculum and in teaching programmes. Also there should be a regular assessment of how far the curriculum in the schools as a whole and for individual pupils matched the stated aims. Since then schools have spent considerable time revising their curricula and have stated their aims in curricular terms in their brochures, as required by the 1980 Education Act. Many special schools have, as part of this exercise, developed excellent leavers' programmes, incorporating elements of independence training, social and lifeskills and work experience. At the same time many colleges of further education have mounted specially designed courses for students with moderate and severe learning difficulties.

There is, however, a need for schools and colleges to work together on a 14-19 curriculum. Leavers' programmes tend to be geared solely towards employment at sixteen years rather than continued education and college courses tend to operate on the 'Let's give them a new start' principle. Whilst the latter may be a laudable sentiment, it negates the knowledge and expertise of the school, wastes valuable time in the reassessment of students' needs and leads to comments already quoted about repetition.

A staff development resource pack, 'From Coping to Confidence', has been developed for further education teachers of students with moderate learning difficulties. It was produced by the Further Education Unit (FEU) and the National Foundation for Educational Research (NFER) for the Department of Education and Science. It comprises seven written modules and an accompanying three-hour video. There is no set method of using the pack, but it is intended for colleges to help themselves to gain background knowledge of learning difficulties, development of a relevant curriculum, teaching styles, student assessment and course evaluation. It is also designed as an in-service tool working towards a whole college approach to students with special educational needs. The pack has a first module introducing ways of working with special needs staff if this is a new experience for staff; it also includes a description of work in special schools. Each module deals with a specific topic, with Module 5 dealing with student negotiation or self-advocacy.

More and more is it being recognised that for the curriculum to be most effective the client must feel to have ownership of it. This theme was developed as part of the FEU's research project called 'Students with Severe Learning Difficulties, RP221'. Students were given a curriculum priority list, the items being discussed individually with the tutor. Aspects of this could then be incorporated into individual programmes.

A recurrent theme of both the Warnock Report and the Education Acts throughout the 1980s has been the importance of parental partnership. Whilst it is recognised that many parents regard the teachers as the experts, many others welcome the opportunity to be involved in the curriculum. Another further education research project, 'Parents as Partners', has taken the idea of curriculum priorities a stage further and made comparisons between student and parent perceptions.

Whether ultimately continued education takes place in school or college, the period from fourteen to nineteen needs to be regarded as a whole. A curriculum framework needs to be drawn up based on local area needs and resources from which an individual school or college can develop its own curriculum. This would include initial assessment, profiling and evaluation. Individual programmes can then be developed by negotiation. Such a framework needs to take account of learning experiences before the age of fourteen years and possible future needs beyond the age of nineteen years.

The LEA must be involved at all stages in the discussion, so that any resource implication can be understood, e.g. staffing levels, both teaching and non-teaching, building and furniture adaptations, specialist equipment and aids, and transport arrangements. Curriculum design and curriculum access must go hand in hand.

## THE OXFORDSHIRE EXPERIENCE

In 1982 two of Oxfordshire's five colleges of further education established courses for students with severe learning disabilities. Since then, and related to a policy decision that all young people should leave special schools at the age of sixteen years, the LEA has encouraged and enabled the development of a programme of provision for all school leavers who have learning difficulties. There now exists a course for students with moderate learning difficulties in each college and provision for students with severe and profound difficulties in three colleges in strategic geographical locations. During the same period there was considerable activity in the special schools focused on two main themes: integration and the curriculum. As a result many schools developed excellent leavers' programmes which involved link courses with their local college.

In the autumn of 1984 a special needs curriculum steering group was formed with representatives from secondary schools, special schools, further education colleges, advisers and educational psychologists, to look at the curriculum for 14-19 students. From this all schools and agencies received a discussion document aimed at stimulating discussion and dialogue on the curriculum issue. A support group for course tutors drawn from all the colleges began to meet together with representatives from the LEA advisory service and local training institutions at least once a term. In 1985 the course tutors' group submitted a request to secure funds from TRIST (TVEI Related In-service Training) for each college and each course to buy time to develop aspects of its own curriculum. This led to each college being given a whole-college topic to tackle. Topics included parents as partners, the 14-19 curriculum for special needs, college management of special needs and a college handbook of special needs. Under the new in-service funding arrangement a 'From Coping to Confidence' trainers' course was mounted for those responsible for special needs in-service within their own college. A three-year scheme, funded by the European Social Fund, has also been running in four colleges to make educational provision available to 18-25-year-old people with special needs. Also in 1984 a joint education, health and social services research project was funded by the Spastic Society to look at the needs of 16-25-year-old physically disabled people.

In 1985 an Oxfordshire joint Education and Social Services Working Party was set up and given the task of identifying the needs and provisions for students who are over 16 years old. One area of decision-making is in relation to funding for students once they have left school and enter into further education. A further problem is the question of how extensive a range of special needs can be catered for in colleges of further education and to what extent students will be part of integrated learning groups. Staffing to support pupils with learning difficulties posed different kinds of problems when considering the needs of the partially sighted or hearing. This year a move has been made to provide peripatetic support service help to the colleges by virtue of the appointment of an educational psychologist with responsibilities for working in the colleges. Steps have also been taken to respond to the Warnock Committee proposals about regional coordination for provision between LEAs. Coordination is also high on the agenda: coordination between colleges in the county as well as coordination and cooperation within individual establishments. Each college has both a special needs in-service coordinator and a named person. Each college is setting up a special needs advisory group and each has an undertaking to produce a statement on the admission of students with special needs.

The outcome of the discussions on 14-19 provision may well lead to the setting up of local curriculum discussion groups combining school and college interests within the new INSET funding arrangements. But if the quality of provision and dialogue is to be improved such issues as paramedical support, common methods of assessment, profiling and recording student progress need to be resolved. Other areas which need to be looked at are alternative teaching methods - experiential, project-based and student-centred - group learning, residential experience and counselling.

## CONCLUSION

Integration can be said to have been achieved when special needs become the concern of all staff, when special needs departments in secondary schools become a resource to all pupils and all staff, when special schools become resource centres for a group of schools, and when staffs of schools and colleges can rightly claim a whole school/college approach to pupils and students with special educational needs.

To achieve this there needs to be a clear intention on behalf of the LEA, a stated policy on behalf of the institutions, a network of discussions between institutions themselves and between institutions and support agencies, which also involves parents and the students, and there needs to be a coordinated programme of in-service training for all staff. Change does not just happen, and neither does it happen rapidly, but the most effective change takes place when those involved have ownership of it. Dialogue and discussion can ensure that it does happen. What is needed is a vision, coordination and flexibility in both attitudes and the deployment of resources. Then the principles and recommendations of the Warnock Report will have been truly embraced.

## REFERENCES

Brockington, D., White, R. and Pring, R. (1985) The 14-18 Curriculum, Bristol: Youth Education Service.

Department of Education and Science (DES) (1978) Special Educational Needs (Warnock Report), London, HMSO.

# PART 3: LEARNING AND THE CURRICULUM

# 8 THE OXFORDSHIRE SKILLS PROGRAMME

John Hanson

## INTRODUCTION

Like many initiatives which gradually gather momentum, resources and their own integrity, the Oxfordshire Skills Programme has a long evolutionary tail.

In the early 1960s the skills of learning to learn were associated, in the classroom, with enquiry methods; they were to be an essential bond in interdisciplinary studies which broke out of the didactic constraints of specialist subjects. There was enthusiasm and invention but, in Oxfordshire as elsewhere, few secondary schools could point to a mastery of those skills. As resource-based learning came to be seen as the pragmatic approach to enquiry and mixed ability work, so a demand arose for study skills. Why do our students not use the library properly? Why do our sixth formers find it difficult to work on their own?

By 1981, there was growing concern that the secondary school curriculum still emphasised the gathering of facts rather than the acquisition of skills. The concern, voiced in the Great Debate initiated by Prime Minister Callaghan, arose partly from extrinsic factors. At a time of economic decline it became more evident that skilled work was essential to our wellbeing as a nation: a utilitarian argument. But skills also gave access to the arts and leisure pursuits, a deterrent against idleness. And not least, skills were enabling, bestowing on their owner a sense of achievement and well-being.

A national conference at Stoke Rochford underlined this concern. Nobody seemed very sure exactly what skills were, but they were certainly a 'good thing'. Lifeskills became part of our vocabulary.

There were a number of reasons why skills had hitherto been held in lower esteem. For example, the term had become associated with craft techniques: a skilled worker used his hands rather than his head. On television, the programme 'Mastermind' beguiled its addicts with the view that intelligence equated with remembering facts. Significantly, in my view, the deference of many university departments to philosophy rather than psychology contributed to a concern for the structure of knowledge at the expense of skills.

In Oxfordshire, the Chief Education Officer, Tim Brighouse, took a strong personal interest in the curricular issue and had attended the Stoke Rochford conference. He established a project which enabled several teachers from five schools to investigate skills in relation to changing curricula. Great difficulty, however, was experienced in probing beyond the skills of enquiry that had become an obligatory part of the introduction to each Schools Council project. What the project soon revealed was the value of school-based secondment to teacher motivation and cooperation. Teachers endeavoured to respond to the challenge in their specialist subject. In history and geography as much as in science and technology, new schemes put a high premium on the skills of the subject. How far these skills represented an exclusive integrity of the subject or a common ground of cognitive skills was not clear.

Edward De Bono came to talk to secondary headteachers about lateral thinking, which was also accepted as a good thing, and two schools later experimented with his published materials.[1] The significant message was that 'thinking' can be learned, can be improved. Yet the practical approach in the classroom seemed often to lack the subtlety and mediation that might be needed to influence learning significantly.

In 1983, Oxfordshire became one of twelve LEAs funded by central government in the Low Achieving Pupils Project, including in its brief a three-year piloting of Instrumental Enrichment. This was another separate approach to thinking skills, based on the work of Reuven Feuerstein (1981) in Israel, in what we would call a special needs context. The scheme is discussed in detail in another chapter. The approach, demanding teacher training, was based on active problem-solving methods, using American materials[2] which proved to be expensive but limited in scope and presentation. The effect upon the chosen teachers involved from five secondary schools however was very positive, due in large part to the excellent training provided by Francis Link of Curriculum Development Associates, Washington DC, USA.

Feuerstein's approach was exceptional in having a firm basis in psychological theory derived, I believe, from his early association with Jean Piaget but placing an important emphasis on the modifiability of cognitive development. It seems essential to me that our educational policies should be underpinned by a psychological theory of learning.

The interpretation of Piaget's influential theories had led to profound changes in Oxfordshire primary school practice in the 1960s, yet had little impact on secondary schools. It is worth speculating on the reasons:

- the emphasis of Piaget's researches was perceived to be with younger children;
- Britain tended to import educational ideas not from Europe but from the United States, where behaviourist views were dominant;
- teacher training reflected a stronger interest in structuring knowledge than in cognitive processes;
- Piaget has not paid much attention to problem-solving outside a limited academic sphere;
- subject specialisation has appeared to conflict with Piaget's holistic theory of cognition.

An end product of our thinking through these varied experiences is, in terms of a separate course approach to cognitive thinking and learning skills, the Oxfordshire Skills Programme. Before outlining some facets of that programme, however, I wish to consider several of the major issues that have arisen. We are still learning.

## WHAT DO WE MEAN BY SKILLS?

We have in our schools a profusion of study skills, learning skills, information skills, enquiry skills, problem-solving skills, lifeskills, skills for self-supported study. There is a problem of definition. No wonder some researchers thought the existence of a skill is itself rather a slippery notion. Robinson (1980), visiting schools to view language work, found that 'skills was a term which I came across many times...and it was a term about which I felt a lot of unease'. Skill is the organisation of our experience that allows effective action, and thinking is a skilled process which, as De Bono indicated, we undertake when we do not know. Cognitive skill enables us to know.

We are in the vicinity of that unfashionable word 'intelligence', the capacity to gain and use knowledge, or as Bruner (1966) put it, 'the power to connect matters that seem separate'.

Butcher (1968) thought that intelligence had become identified with convergent and creativity with divergent thinking. In any case he considered motivation a greatly underrated factor. Modgil and Modgil (1976) referred to two possible levels of Piagetian formal operations: problem-solving and problem-finding, the latter perhaps characterising creative thought. Gardner (1984) presented evidence for seven distinct human intelligences, though he was ready to accept an overriding general ability.

There may be as many definitions as there are psychologists. I take cognitive skills to be the organisation of experience that leads to 'knowing how' and 'knowing that'. This is consistent with Piaget's constructionist theory by which everything derives from actions and is eventually translated into coherent and logical thought operations. Creativity is surely the ability to see new problems, relationships and solutions, a project of logic or of imagination.

Our objectives are related to the formal stage of operations in Piagetian terms, a stage which Modgil and Modgil (1976) noted 'has received relatively little empirical attention'. The theoretical ground is still open to argument. Piaget identified the transition from concrete to formal operations with a facility to identify and devise alternatives, to organise strategies to meet many possibilities in a situation, to formulate and describe hypotheses, to draw conclusions by inference, to find relationships between factors, to identify invariant factors, to predict and test consequences, to devise procedures, to dissociate form from content.

Failure to acquire such skills puts a student at a great disadvantage in secondary school where much teaching and many textbooks assume a formal level of operations. It is relevant to the teacher's wide role that failure sometimes stems from social factors, such as the language of the home or anxiety arising from personal relationships, and may in time be compounded by emotional blocks. Some teachers will say: 'Adapt the approach in the classroom for those incapable of higher levels of thinking.' I believe that students may be capable of much more.

## ARE THE SKILLS TEACHABLE?

A variety of research has indicated that at least 50 per cent of fifteen-year-olds fail to manifest formal thinking, which Piaget, perhaps working too often with bright Genevan children, thought developed normally between the ages of 12 and 15 years. Uncertainty on this issue led Dulit (1972) to describe the formal stage at adolescence as a 'characteristic potentiality' rather than reality. Can teaching realise that potential?

When the 1945 Norwood Report referred to 'the grammar school mind...interested in learning for its own sake...it can take in an argument...is interested in causes', it implied an immutable ability. You either had it or you hadn't.

The issue of whether cognitive skills can be enhanced by teaching can also be approached from the question of whether intelligence is an immutable factor. This was indeed the view of early psychologists, but recent research and thinking has indicated a plasticity, most marked in the earliest years of childhood but evident too in adolescence. If cognitive development can be modified, then potential is increased. Both the Robbins and Newsom reports stressed that intelligence was not an immutable factor. More recently, researches in psychology and neurology have added further weight to the argument that an enriched environment seems to stimulate intellectual ability and may compensate for earlier deficiency.

Piaget's stance was cautious. 'If it be true that all structures are generated, it is just as true that generation is always a passing from a simpler to a more complex structure, this process according to the present state of knowledge being endless.'

Donaldson (1978) suggested that 'there is no reason to suppose that most of us - or any of us for that matter - manage to come close to realising what we are capable of. And it is not even certain that it makes a great deal of sense to think in terms of upper limits at all.'

Lovell (1971) reported that 'studies of language...suggest that family life style has implications for cognitive development'. The language of the middle-class home was more likely than that of the working-class home to be hypothetical and reflective. 'Much could be done by families...to help their children acquire and use in diverse situations those thinking skills which are now increasingly demanded by developed and developing societies. Should teachers involve parents in their schemes?

There is a range of research studies[3] mostly with young children, supporting the argument that training can enhance cognitive development. Clinical studies tend, however, to be some distance from the classroom, often conducted with privileged children of a Western urban culture. Few schemes to teach thinking skills in schools have been thoroughly evaluated; the difficulties are numerous. Hunter-Grundin's (1985) evaluation of De Bono's materials in primary schools was largely negative, but may simply indicate that too young an age group was involved.

Although Weller and Craft's (1983) early findings on schools' use of Feuerstein's Instrumental Enrichment gave as many reasons for concern as for encouragement, Feuerstein (1981) claimed considerable success with adolescents in Israel. His strategies were 'to assist the child in the acquisition of concepts, operations and strategies; to encourage intrinsic motivation; to provide insight into the causes of success and failure; and to transform the individual from a passive recipient of information into an active generator and extrapolator of ideas'. His claims have yet to be fully evaluated in this country.

The Oxfordshire Skills Programme takes cognisance of both Piaget and Feuerstein, and hope from the arguments of Donaldson, in proposing tutor-led approaches where sensitive mediation encourages student insight, diagnostic assessment and, not least, rigorous study habits. If we accept that there are fewer limits to potential than we have hitherto been ready to assume, the message holds true for teachers too.

## IS THERE TRANSFER?

The extent to which transfer of learning occurs, in the sense of learned skills and concepts being applied to new problems, is a measure of the effectiveness of learning. Many assumptions are made; thus syllabuses call for an emphasis on developing skills in a way which enables the learner to transfer them from one context to another. But the fact is that little is known of methods which facilitate transfer. On the other hand, transfer must occur or learning could not progress.

Bruner (1966) took an optimistic view: 'It is indeed a fact that massive general transfer can be achieved by appropriate learning, even to the degree that learning properly under optimum conditions leads one to "learn how to learn".' Does the idea of transfer of skill imply a general form of ability? Butcher (1968) suggested that such general ability must have common factors in its wide range of performances and also an integrating function involving superior powers of selection and coordination. This was consistent with Spearman's G factor. Some psychologists, however, have argued for a range of virtually autonomous domains and no effective transfer. This question is critical to the argument for a separate 'thinking skills' course as opposed to building elements into specialised subjects.

Piaget's view of cognitive development is essentially holistic. He has, however, acknowledged:

> only moderately sized correlations in the application of common strategies to different tasks; that the transfer of general abilities to particular subject areas seems to be affected by the student's interest and knowledge in the subject; that a range of constraints appears to operate on transfer.

One wonders whether developmental aspects are significant and whether subject areas may acquire a greater autonomy at adolescence through diversification of aptitude or in appearance only by school emphasis on subject specialisation. Certainly the acquisition of skills in the context of subject-specific language and concepts is likely to inhibit transfer and give an impression of autonomy.

My opinion is that while students' interests and

experience are strong influences and motivators in performance, and particular aptitudes may be evident, there is a general area of cognitive development to be enriched. Little evidence of transfer was indicated in the early evaluation in this country of work based on the programmes of De Bono or Feuerstein, though it was noted that few teachers involved sought to achieve it.

Kahney (1986) expressed surprise that 'if people are left to themselves, they are not good at bringing their previous experience to bear in solving related problems'. Other researchers indicated the need for careful structuring of problems and for teacher intervention.

My own view, based on task analysis, is that too little attention has been given to essential prior knowledge and to motivation for transfer, while the territorial imperative of subject departments may be a strongly inhibiting factor. We should probably be considering at least three forms of transfer: concept formation or association, horizontal (cross-curricular) transfer, and vertical (more difficult tasks in the same mode) transfer. I have recently seen the need to emphasise operational ability as the key to transfer, that ability coming from a mastery of cognitive skills processes, each process being a compound of cognitive skills. The hierarchy of skill that emerges is vital to assessment.

We seek a fuller understanding of skill. Much more rigorous work needs to be done in schools and colleges to provide hard evidence. At present it seems reasonable for tutors to provide a focus for mediated cognitive skills learning as one aspect of personal development, knowing that teachers as subject specialists must have a keen interest in the application of those skills and procedures. It should be a shared concern.

There are several reasons why the tutor should invest the learning skills in his or her pastoral curriculum:

- to foster personal and social development (including 'effective thinking');
- to facilitate diagnostic assessment and guidance for success;
- to promote 'reasonable' attitudes and routines;
- to encourage the self-reliance needed for self-supported study and independent work;
- to promote achievement rather than failure.

## THE OXFORDSHIRE SKILLS PROGRAMME

This programme is concerned with the development of thinking skills, the development of teachers' formative guidance, and students' autonomy in learning. It seeks the skill of the reasonable person, who listens, observes, questions, considers the available evidence, makes a judgement which he or she is ready to justify, modify in the light of new ideas and act upon, combining clear thinking with fairmindedness. It seeks the skill of the capable person, who has know-how across major areas of experience, including the aesthetic and social; it seeks, at an appropriate stage, the skill of the knowledgeable person, who knows about ideas and is motivated to explore them beyond their utilitarian value, finding pleasure and fulfilment in the process.

It is probable that we cannot teach the skills of thinking any more than, as Polanyi (1958) illustrated, we can teach anyone to swim. We are concerned with the best environment for their tacit learning. In this, assessment becomes a formative, diagnostic tool for improving learning. The teacher's formative guidance may be instrumental in helping individual students to overcome their various difficulties and achieve autonomy, the ability to think for themselves, and study effectively on their own.

The Programme seeks to achieve its aims by:

- encouraging talk and negotiation;
- encouraging the language of thinking and associating that language with the thinking process rather than immediately with a subject context;
- providing a structure for problem-solving and decision-making;
- reducing the factual content in skills learning to focus on the process;
- enabling success;
- providing active guidance by the teacher;
- encouraging feedback from the students;
- giving insight into individual performance.

The content of the Programme might be listed, at the cognitive skills level, as perception, concepts, comparing, classification, analysis, estimation, deduction and synthesis; at a process level as formulation, planning, evaluation, application and decision-making. But, whatever the immediate nature of the task in hand, a high premium is placed on the whole operation of problem-solving, that is, on operational ability and the teacher's incisive role in mediating between the student's experience and his task.

Let me now try to illustrate the Programme in action. A teaching session begins with the teacher showing a brick. He may tease the group by suggesting he found it growing in his garden or that it fell from outer space - a meteorite. He asks: What is it? Describe it. What is its name? Why do we name things? The teacher leads the discussion further, building on previous work.

What makes you think it is a brick? What can be said about this brick which is true of all bricks? What attributes must an object have to be named 'brick'? What things about a brick are universal?

Discussion, drawing on the student's experience, soon reveals that bricks may not all be red, nor have six sides, nor a standard size. A dictionary aids discussion. The teacher will try to draw out a recognition that 'brick' is a concept which varies with historical age and culture.

In a pair the student may now attempt to define the idea of 'brick' - perhaps 'a block of regular shape, light enough to lift in one hand, which is used for building'. The attempts are reviewed in turn, criticised, justified. Eventually, a consensus is sought - the rules for 'brick'.

The teacher may now introduce objects or overhead projection drawings to test the new rule. Is this a brick? Is that a brick? Does it fit our agreed definition? Does our definition itself stand up to the test?

Thus far the teacher will be covering ideas already met in considering concepts and perception. Now he introduces the idea of 'form'. What does it mean? What does the dictionary say? What is the form of this brick? Why does it have that form? Particularly with larger student groups, some questions may best be put to students in twos or fours in order to get fuller participation.

A forty-minute session would be drawn to a close by the teacher asking some or all members of the group to respond to a question. Either 'What did we learn in this lesson?' or 'What was the best and worst part of today's lesson?' Such feedback is important not only for consolidation and the teacher's self-appraisal but also for the students' sense of negotiating the process of learning, the opportunity to listen to what others have to say, to summarise and express clearly their own feelings.

The next lesson is based on a worksheet. The subject is perception of form, the objective to perceive accurately a given rectangle lying within a complex field. The teacher's aim is to develop awareness of strategies for finding the rectangle, the need to be accurate and to check work, to discover and mediate on any difficulties exhibited by individuals in perception.

The worksheet may best be introduced on an overhead projector to discourage impulsive starters. The teacher asks: What can be seen on this sheet? Describe it. A system of reference needs to be adopted so that communication can be made easier.

The teacher establishes through discussion that there are no obvious instructions but that the task is implicit. The heavy line of the rectangle may be taken as a cue. Agreement is reached that we are to find that same shape in each of the other frames.

What is the shape? Can we call it a brick? A box? A rectangle? Why is 'rectangle' the best name? What are the universal rules for a rectangle? What do the dictionaries tell us?

The teacher leads more questions, the students working in pairs: what is the form of the rectangle? Which attributes are going to help us find the rectangle in the other frames? Which should we look for first? Suggestions come back. No right answer is indicated.

Is the task going to get easier or harder as we work down the page? Separate worksheets present the same task at a remedial and a more difficult level. We may need to adapt our strategy as we proceed to more difficult frames.

When the sheet is distributed, students may start work individually upon it. As students work, the teacher moves among them, noting individuals that operate with obvious mastery or difficulty, seeking to draw out from the latter the cause of their difficulty and a means to success. Students who finish first may give help to others or go on to a more difficult sheet to be finished as homework.

Review is an important part of the lesson. The purpose of the task is not to show who can do it and who cannot, but to find how everyone can find a means of succeeding. Discussion thus ranges over the task, which frames were easiest, or hardest, and why. The success of various strategies is considered. The likelihood is recognised of using a 'pop-out' strategy because it works in the second frame of the top row but then foundering in later frames, bereft of other strategies. Who changed their strategy? Concern for accuracy is encouraged. Who can suggest occasions when accuracy can be a matter of life or death? The last five minutes are given to feedback, underlining the value of thinking before tackling a task.

The teacher will be anxious to diagnose any problems in visual perception, for these could indicate an underlying cause of learning difficulty. But the lesson as a whole focuses on operational ability and a student involvement that may lead them to restructure their experience.

A final thought is that teachers, working with ideas that may be unfamiliar to parents and developing language that may be very different from that of the home, may wisely bring parents in to a discussion of the course and its objectives.

## SUMMARY

The Oxfordshire Skills Programme has drawn on many sources over a number of years, particularly on the ideas of Piaget and Feuerstein. Our practice, research and development have not, I hope, led us to a new rigid orthodoxy, for the price of true progress is constant revision. We are still learning and our materials may never reach a final draft.

What we have already experienced has brought us closer to the heart of our professional role as teachers, for what can be more important than our ability to recognise and overcome students' learning difficulties? Any success will help us to refine our professional skill in assessing and supporting students in their learning and self-evaluation. I am encouraged in this by colleagues who say, 'I myself am a better teacher as a result of this experience.'

## NOTES

1. De Bono's materials were published as the CORT Thinking Programme (1981) by Oxford University Press.

2. Instrumental Enrichment materials were published by University Park Press, 300 North Charles Street, Baltimore, Maryland 21201, and disseminated by Curriculum Development Associates, Suite 404, 1211 Connecticut Avenue, Washington DC 20036.
3. The Oxfordshire Skills Project materials are being produced by the Education Unit, Wheatley Centre, Littleworth Road, Wheatley, Oxfordshire OX9 1PH.

## REFERENCES


Bruner, J. (1966) Towards a Theory of Instruction, Cambridge: Harvard University Press.

Butcher, H. (1968) Human Intelligence, London: Methuen.

Donaldson, M. (1978) Children and Their Thinking, London: Fontana.

Dulit, M. (1972) 'Adolescent thinking à la Piaget', Youth Adolescent Journal, 3.

Feuerstein, R. (1981) Instrumental Enrichment, Baltimore University Press.

Gardner, H. (1984) Frames of Mind, London: Heinemann.

Hunter-Grundin, E. (1985) An Evaluation of the Classroom Materials of Edward De Bono, London: Schools Council.

Kahney, H. (1986) Problem Solving: A Cognitive Approach, Milton Keynes: Open University Press.

Lovell, K. (1971) Educational Psychology and Children, London: University of London Press.

Modgil, M. and Modgil, A. (1976) Piagetian Research Windsor: NFER.

Newsom, J. (196 ), Half Our Future, London, HMSO.

Norwood Report (1943) Secondary Schools Examination Council, London: HMSO.

Polanyi, M. (1973) Personal Knowledge, London: Routledge & Kegan Paul.

Robinson, I. (1980) Language Across the Curriculum, London: Schools Council and Methuen.

Weller, K. and Craft, A. (1983) Making Up Our Minds, London: Schools Council.

# 9 OPEN AND INTERACTIVE LEARNING: THE LAP PROGRAMME

Patrick Leeson

## INTRODUCTION

This chapter is an attempt to set out the nature of the problems for pupils' learning that Oxfordshire's response to the LAP Programme - the New Learning Initiative - is intended to address, and the viewpoints about teaching and learning on which it is founded. A particular focus is on the question of pupils' thinking and understanding, and the teaching of specific thinking skills courses, such as Feuerstein's Instrumental Enrichment and the Oxfordshire Skills Programme. The main argument concerns the need for more interactive approaches to learning, to emphasise the centrality of pupils' own thinking and understanding and the need for more use of fundamental concept-forming processes in learning.

### The new learning initiative

In 1982, Sir Keith Joseph, Secretary of State for Education and Science, announced a programme of government funded development projects designed to put into practice, and to evaluate, new approaches to the education of lower attaining pupils, especially in the last two years of compulsory education. The overall aim was to improve the educational attainment of pupils for whom existing examinations at 16+ are not appropriate and those whose general experience of school is one of failure and disaffection. One of the ways to achieve this, it was suggested, would be to shift pupils' education away from the narrowly conceived courses and teaching styles, to approaches more suited to their needs, and to give a practical slant to much of what is taught.

HMI identified three means by which such change might come about:

- by experiment with teaching contexts or environments;
- by experiment with teaching methods and approaches;
- by more accurate identification of needs and the responses appropriate to those needs.

HMI also referred to a fundamental difficulty in the nature of the project: the difficulty of identifying so-called lower attaining pupils and defining which pupils we are in fact talking about. In simple terms:

> The bottom 40 per cent was chosen because CSE officially caters roughly for the eightieth down to the fortieth percentile of ability [but this] does not assume that pupils' attainment will be constant across the range of examination subjects (if they are taken) still less across the range of un-examined challenges or tasks that might be set within the school curriculum ... Over the whole of a pupil's school career his or her performance can fluctuate markedly and unpredictably. Pupils do not necessarily remain in one category of ability.

Accordingly the pupils we are talking about could include pupils whom we call slow learners and whose general ability is well below average; pupils with specific learning difficulties who are not necessarily the least able but who are unsuccessful in terms of how we measure school success; pupils who have persistent learning difficulties due to physical impairment and emotional problems; and pupils who are not necessarily included in any kind of special needs provision but whose needs are given less attention than the obviously more or less able.

HMI offered the following working definition: lower attaining pupils in Year 4 and 5 for whom present examinations at 16+ are not designed, including not only those of below average ability, but also those whose low attainments are not necessarily due to low ability or particular learning difficulties, and those other pupils whose low attainments might be improved by access to more effective styles of teaching and learning. The clearest direction, then, at the outset was to develop the kind of curriculum provision that is capable of responding to the needs of individual pupils, no matter who they are and whatever their needs.

## The lower attaining pupils' project in Oxfordshire

By definition, this kind of project begs important questions about the nature of school failure and educational attainment. Once we begin to look at pupils and what they are like we have to ask 'what are the real problems? Do they reside with the pupils or with the curriculum and organisation of the school, or both?'

### Background

The major structural and organisational changes that came with comprehensivisation in the 1960s and 1970s have not resulted in the kind of improvements in equal opportunity and access to knowledge that were envisaged. The dominant understanding of ability, and of the problems of those who supposedly have a lack of it, remains narrow and erroneous. Access to knowledge and therefore more equal opportunity are still often restricted on the grounds of this narrow concept of ability, with the result that the 14-16 curriculum is frequently uniform and inflexible. The academic subject curriculum, so goes the familiar argument, determines the whole structure of many schools and the experience of all pupils. This inflexibility, and the misleading notions about youngsters' ability and intellectual development, which are some of the most obvious features of the secondary curriculum, mean that the cut-off points for what counts as good learning and appropriate responses are too narrowly defined for large numbers of pupils. These pupils then become problems and can usually be relied on to exhibit the typical characteristics we associate with low attainers, including disruptive behaviour, hostility, reluctance to learn, negative attitudes to school, truancy, passive withdrawal, poor motivation, lack of confidence and low self-esteem, as well as specific learning difficulties.

## The deficient pupil model

One explanation is to regard these pupils as fundamentally deficient and their failure at school as inevitable. Their abilities are limited because they lack intelligence. They do not meet standards and they do their work badly because they do not understand it and will never master certain concepts and skills. The only thing to be done with them is to decide what their appropriate needs are and give them only what we think they can master. In other words we should not make the same demands on them as we make on more able children. Instead we should water down their learning so that they can cope, and give them an alternative curriculum to suit their limitations.

These views have come to dominate thinking in education so powerfully and pervasively that it is sometimes difficult to consider the alternatives. They are derived from the overwhelming influence of psychometrics and behaviourism in psychological theory, which views intelligence as an innate capacity which is static and fixed, and can be measured. The corresponding theory of knowledge derives from the long tradition of empiricism, in which knowledge is viewed as something external and factual, to be discovered, with objective rules and laws. Intelligence is the innate capacity to receive this knowledge.

Our notions of teaching and learning, based on these views, seem rather straightforward. Knowledge is something to be transmitted to those who are capable of receiving it. Teaching is didactic, there are right and wrong answers to most questions, the teacher knows his or her body of knowledge and the precise norms and standards to be met. The overriding purpose is to meet the demands of the particular subject's knowledge content.

## The deficient school model

An alternative explanation for many of the problems represented by lower-attaining pupils is that like anybody else they have active and curious minds, but that schools fail to engage those minds in subjectively meaningful ways. Common complaints from many pupils include:

- I never get the chance to do anything that interests me.

- I just don't see the point of a lot of what we do in lessons.
- Nothing is ever explained so it makes sense.
- I never get enough help in lessons.
- No matter how hard I try I'm still no good.

What comments of this kind really mean is that teaching is not interactive enough, that not enough value is attached to pupils' own ideas and experience, that there is not enough choice and say in what is learned and that there are few situations where pupils recognise a need to learn. If we are to make a serious attempt to translate such criticisms into different patterns of teaching and learning we need fundamentally to alter our theoretical viewpoint, our concepts of knowledge and ability.

An alternative, and more useful, notion of intelligence is that, far from being something which is a single and fixed ability, it is a developing interactive entity made up of many abilities which adapt to environment and experience. This makes it very difficult to predict and measure what individuals are capable of, and it makes the whole business of getting hold of knowledge much more open-ended and problematic.

Inevitably this changes our notions about the status and nature of knowledge which, if our minds actively construct and change it and perceive its meanings differently, itself becomes problematic and questionable. Facts are not immutable, and the context and purpose of knowledge will always matter for the individual's understanding. In other words the overriding purpose for education in this theoretical framework is the demand to reach and develop every individual's understanding, in ways which are meaningful for him or her.

The implications for teaching and learning are significant: we need to start where the pupil's needs and understanding are; learning must have an obvious purpose and relevance; experience matters and the environment we provide for learning needs to provide many different contexts and stimuli; concepts are grasped through activity and active participation, and knowledge must be used; pupils must not be told so much but rather should learn through investigation and deduction; and the significance of any learning has to be viewed more in terms of the pupil's perspective and subjective understanding.

If we put these different positions side by side we might see the nature of the problem more clearly.

| Traditional | Progressive |
|---|---|
| Knowledge centred | Child centred |
| Fixed intellectual capacity | Intelligence develops through response to direct experience |
| Facts, ideas, need to be put in for child to develop | The environment is important |
| The mind is a blank sheet | The mind is naturally disposed to learn |
| The child is passive | The child is active/ intelligent |
| The adult imposes meaning | The adult guides/ encourages and informs, organises, suggests, instructs |
| Norms and standards are fixed | The child's own tendencies matter, therefore she/he needs freedom |
| The child who fails is deficient | The child can develop on her/his own initiative. Schooling stimulates the process |
| The child needs adult/ instructor to develop | The focus is on activity/interest |
| Emphasis: cultural transmission, what society needs | Emphasis: the child's own needs |

These two viewpoints appear to be irreconcilable, although both may coexist and operate together in the thinking and practice of many teachers. The usual pedagogical response is to respect the knowledge-centred curriculum, and to either neglect, ignore or remove from it those pupils who experience difficulty, and to provide for them an alternative and more child-centred provision in special needs, non-examination classes and disruptive units.

When we expand our notions of achievement and ability, and attempt to make the curriculum more flexible and learning more open-ended, then the cut-off points for success and failure change significantly and become rather more blurred. This shift in emphasis requires our pedagogy to be more interactive and pupil-centred for all pupils. In other words the main focus becomes the organisation of the curriculum and the nature and quality of classroom interaction. In spite of the many explanations for school failure in terms of class and cultural disadvantage, linguistic deficiency and the social functions of schooling, which one would not want to reject, there is now also an attempt to look more closely at the nature of pupil-teacher interaction in the classroom as the source of difficulty with learning and its remediation.

## THE NEW LEARNING INITIATIVE

The Lower Attaining Pupils Programme in Oxfordshire is known as the New Learning Initiative. This project has set out to redefine concepts of ability and, through certain curricular activities, teaching styles and open and interactive learning methods, to expand and develop what counts for attainment in schools.

Some of the main characteristics of the Initiative are:

- an open classroom approach to learning which enlists the active help of others in the wider community;
- an open school approach which recognises the importance of 'off-site' community-based learning and a curriculum which is developed accordingly;
- an emphasis on negotiated learning which explores attitudes, skills, concepts and experience through experiment and problem-solving;
- the promotion of pupils' active participation and decision-making in their own learning, and opportunities for genuine pupil feedback and

evaluation;
- the development of structured oral work and group work as a central strategy in enquiry-based learning;
- the need for good differentiation in teaching approaches which provides for individualised learning and responds sensitively to the needs of individual pupils.

The three main curricular activities through which open and interactive learning are substantially promoted are: school-community links; residential education; and instrumental enrichment.

Although the intention has been to promote change across the curriculum and to have a whole school impact, the sharp focus on these three areas of activity is attractive for many reasons:

- they are an alternative to narrowly conceived traditional education;
- they value and respect a wide range of abilities and experiences that pupils have;
- no known limits are placed on pupils' potential;
- they attack the notion of learning as simply the accumulation of ideas and facts that are important to society;
- they promote the idea of learning as the development of skills that are important to the individual;
- they hope to liberate children from some of the inhibiting and destructive aspects of schooling;
- the pupil is not viewed as imperfect or deficient;
- the pupil is not a passive receiver but she/he must actively construct the meaning of her or his world by perceiving and doing.

Since all children are not equally alert, active, curious explorers of their world and, as might be expected, seem unable to learn from all sorts of direct experiences, the demands made on teaching are numerous and complex. Pupils need to learn the strategies and habits, and the systems of thought, that we use to make sense of the world. They need to learn how to learn. For a model of teaching and learning that is demonstrably about teaching people to learn and to think we must look at the cognitive education programme known as Instrumental Enrichment and the work of Reuven Feuerstein.

## Instrumental Enrichment

In simple terms Instrumental Enrichment (IE) teaches 'thinking about thinking' and 'learning about learning' rather than any specific subject matter. It claims to assess and correct the cognitive deficiencies that impair intellectual functioning and result in the poor performance of those whom Feuerstein calls culturally deprived. This refers, not to the lack of any specific culture but to the lack of particular experiences in development which are essential to the child's learning about the world and his relation with it.

The culture of the family and the social group is mediated - organised, selected, explained and filtered - through the intervention of parents or caring adults and when this breaks down the child is deprived of the ability to learn from experience. Feuerstein describes this as lack of what he called Mediated Learning Experience. His theory of cognitive modifiability, which explains this syndrome, claims that the level of intellectual functioning of any individual and her/his control of the processes of thought are always open to change and improvement. It is the purpose of IE to restore the ability to learn from fresh experience, and it is this contribution of Feuerstein's - a range of structured teaching materials and a definite method for teaching - apart from his theoretical analysis, which opens up new possibilities for the successful teaching and learning of pupils with learning difficulties.

For many years there has been doubt about the primacy of genetic control over intellectual performance, and a growing body of opinion holds that slow thinking and learning are the results of an unsuitable development process.

Several authors have argued that cognitive functioning can be positively or negatively influenced by one's environment (De Bono, 1970, 1973, 1976; Feuerstein, 1981) and have put forward programmes for improving thinking skills. Feuerstein differs from, say, De Bono, in claiming that this kind of intervention not only improves habits and strategies for thinking and learning, but alters in a fundamentally structural way the cognitive processes that underlie intellectual capacity. IE is not a skill-training or 'deficit' model but a meta-cognitive approach aimed at generalising the strategies and abilities from particular situations to the level of conscious awareness and control of one's own learning.

The emphasis on cognitive processes - the way the child perceives the world, processes information and communicates the results - uncovers a variety of learning problems which allow for the intervention to be targeted at specific features of thought processes. Apart from the lack of familiarity with content, difficulty with the communication mode used in learning, the nature and amount of information involved, the level of abstraction and the speed and precision with which an individual operates, specific problems can occur in any or all of three phases: information gathering; elaboration or solution finding; and output, the process of communicating to oneself and to others the solution to the problem.

A child may experience major problems with one particular phase - and it seems likely that many school pupils who are impulsive and unsystematic have difficulty with information gathering - yet they may be treated, inappropriately, as if the problem lies elsewhere or as if a more general problem exists.

The deficiencies which result from poor mediation can be categorised as the negative aspects of these specific thought processes: for example, blurred and sweeping perception at the input stage; inadequacy in experiencing and defining a task or a problem during the elaboration phase; imprecise and idiosyncratic use of language at the output phase.

Feuerstein defines cognitive functions as 'process variables that are themselves compounds of native ability, attitude, work habits, learning history, motives, and strategies' (Smith et al., 1982). The attempt to organise specific cognitive deficiencies in terms of a division of the mental act into three phases is intended to bring some order to the variety of impairments that can occur in learning and thinking, and to their remediation in the classroom.

## IE in the classroom

Feuerstein's programme (IE), designed to deal with cognitive and motivational difficulties, comprises fourteen sets, or instruments, of exercises which are largely free of specific academic subject matter. Each instrument is intended to provide opportunities for defining and solving particular kinds of problems, with intensive mediation by the teacher, to compensate for missed mediated experience, and to change the pupil's thinking ability. The decontextualised exercises are designed to be intrinsically motivating, and, although highly structured, are intended to make learning open-ended and interdisciplinary.

For example, the instruments include the Organisation of Dots, where the pupil has to work systematically and accurately to figure out the rules of organisation in order to solve the problem. The goals of this instrument are clearly defined and can help the teacher to mediate for a number of the specific aspects of thinking through the problems: for example, the projection of virtual (implied) relationship; definition and labelling of forms; analysis of differences among characteristics of different but similar forms; the internal representation and mental transformation of forms from different orientations; systematic search strategies; planning; use of cues; comparison, use of standard model; self-checking and spontaneous correction; precision and accuracy; and principles of organisation.

Another instrument is called Comparisons and is intended to teach spontaneous comparative behaviour and to provide a basis for classification. This instrument does not assume that pupils are unable to compare but that they do not compare spontaneously. They look at reality in an episodic and fragmented way because no one has mediated appropriately to help them see relationships between wholes and parts. The teaching goals of Comparisons include teaching the use of precise descriptive terms; spontaneous comparison; alternative dimensions of comparing; determination of relevant and irrelevant aspects; identifying difference and similarity; distinction between perceptual and semantic characteristics; the continuum of concrete to abstract characteristics; and grouping by definitions.

Other instruments are called Analytic Perception, Orientation in Space, Categorisation, Family Relationships, Numerical Progression and Instructions. Higher level units deal with syllogistic thinking and formal propositional logic in Transitive Relations and Syllogism.

The materials are used only after the teacher has introduced certain concepts and discussed their relation to particular situations and problems from as many different perspectives as possible. The pupils then seek strategies to solve the problems on the page and are taught to organise their ideas and to work systematically. They learn to assess their own ideas and actions, and are encouraged to look for wider connections for specific concepts in their general experience and other areas of learning. This process is known as bridging and involves the teacher and pupils in discussing ways in which specific experiences in IE can be generalised, that is, ways in which events and ideas that seem separate can be connected, which is one of Bruner's (1966) ways of describing intelligence. How well we make these connections determines our capacity as thinkers.

The important question for IE and for other areas of the curriculum is to ask: what are the processes, in pupil-teacher interaction, which provide the right kind of experiences to overcome deficiencies and improve cognitive performance and motivation? Apart from the IE materials, or the subject matter of other areas of learning, what should we be doing in teaching and learning? Feuerstein uses the term 'mediation' to describe the ways in which we interact purposefully and creatively with the learner.

## Mediation

Mediated Learning Experience is the term used to describe the necessary interactions that facilitate the response by the learner to direct experience (Feuerstein, 1981). The conditions, or different kinds of mediation, which Feuerstein describes are a very useful way of looking more closely at the essential and important features of any pupil-teacher interaction.

Piaget says that something very decisive happens in early adolescence, which is the capacity to reason verbally in terms of hypotheses and no longer merely in terms of concrete objects. To reason hypothetically is a formal reasoning process which subordinates the real to the possible and goes beyond the immediate. This changes the nature of learning, and discussion, and makes new demands. To adopt another's point of view, to draw 'other' consequences, and to become interested in problems which go beyond the immediate field of experience involves the learner in constructing theories, elaborating on the significance of events and ideas, and understanding ideologies and systems. Language and communication play an increasingly important role in this process of intellectual growth. The receptive and productive powers of language, vocabulary, command of structure and logical rigour, especially in the verbal medium, are very important for intellectual growth to proceed in the direction of more hypothetical thinking.

For example, when a child is learning how to organise the elements of his environment into classes of widening generality and abstraction, it is not simply about labels and vocabulary but about how to select from them to form new concepts. Concept formation does not arise out of 'instances' or isolated events, but out of whole contexts. This takes language beyond recalling the simple referent or usage-meaning of words to the wider and greyer areas of meaning and understanding. In other words what is called for is a range of cognitive activity, through language, which includes inferential thought, analogy, interpretation and translation, and invoking knowledge from outside. These language-directed cognitive processes underlie all subject-matter understanding and they place the emphasis in teaching and learning on the quality of communication, and relationships between, teacher and pupils.

Feuerstein (1981) describes the different aspects of this communication, or mediation, in the following way. The criteria of mediated learning experiences are:

- intentionality and reciprocity
- transcendence
- mediation and meaning
- mediation of feeling of competence
- mediated regulation and control of behaviour
- mediated sharing behaviour
- mediated individuation and psychological differentiation
- mediation of goal seeking, goal setting and goal achieving planning behaviour
- mediation of challenge: the search for novelty and complexity

The three essential elements of pupil-teacher interaction here are the sharing of its intention to initiate a specific activity and need for the learner; the need to aim at remote goals and to transcend the meaning of immediate problems to anticipated events and future horizons; and the need to 'negotiate' and search for the shared meaning and significance of words, ideas and events.

Other criteria include the need for the teacher/mediator to make the child feel that she or he is able and competent, and to regulate behaviour and pace the learning so that the child becomes more autonomous and more in control. These conditions are necessary for all mediated learning interactions, and it is through the process of mediated learning that the child becomes a social being and an able learner.

In this way IE, and other approaches to learning which are explicitly interactive, explore open responses and the grey areas in thought and language so as to focus on what is really going on in children's understanding. General education is too often concerned with closed responses, that is, not with what originates in the learners. They then do not elaborate, do not bring their own ideas so readily to the task and do not have to check and evaluate their own responses. Therefore, learning does not bring children to the edge of their current understanding. The teacher controls and organises this process, a verbal and negotiated process as far as possible, because even when situations are not encased in language the process of generalising and understanding is characterised by verbalised concepts.

What we are saying, then, is that the dynamic of teaching and learning should be essentially problem-orientated, language-centred and should be mostly about the individual pupil's own explanations, concept formation and application of established ideas to new situations. Instrumental Enrichment provides a detailed practical and theoretical model for this approach to learning. Leaving aside whether one accepts Feuerstein's claims that intellectual functioning can be modified in a fundamentally structural way, we are left with a more process-orientated view of learning which does not have sharply defined cut-off points for pupils with learning difficulties. Learning is viewed as a continuum which is not primarily concerned with subject matter understanding but with concept formation and how the subject matter is being represented and interpreted by the learner. Any subject matter is then problematic because it is always a question of how the child perceives and understands it, and her/his awareness of how the understanding comes about.

This argument is not just concerned with the need for

a specific cognitive skills course like IE, which is largely stripped of subject matter, but also with the need for a greater emphasis to be placed on cognitive education across the curriculum in all areas of subject matter learning. It is frequently the case that too much subject matter does away with questions of elaboration, explanation and interpretation, that is, with enough thinking and understanding, which leads to confusion and disorientation for many pupils. To get to higher levels of thought which are capable of representing realities which are absent, in other words to be able to use knowledge effectively, we have to learn how to organise and classify, form concepts, explain, interpret and reinterpret, and we need to experience these processes as directly and explicitly as possible.

## Demands on learning

One of the most radical demands on learning, as a result, is the need to escape established ideas about fixedness of knowledge and, instead, to identify key concepts in order to suggest content. This in turn demands a major change of viewpoint for many teachers' assumptions about knowledge and understanding. The curriculum needs to be more child-centred, individuated, open-ended and negotiable, and there should be an explicit focus on language

- to explore thinking,
- to form concepts, and
- to assess understanding.

Learning should make more use of fundamental concept-forming processes, which in turn means finding the starting point for pupils, what they know and do not know, and then teaching from there. We need a methodology which encourages opinions, propositions and judgement-making, the use of conflicting evidence and the exploration of uncertainty and ambiguity. The important question for IE, and other thinking skills programmes, and for all areas of learning is how to put together, in a pupil-centred way, particular concepts and skills with appropriate subject matter and with appropriate pacing.

One outcome of the attempt to put attitudes and individuals' perceptions at the centre of learning is to draw together the so-called pastoral and academic elements of the curriculum. Getting pupils to think, to be aware, and to make decisions implies a 'pastoral' role for all teaching, and for all teachers, and an explicit cognitive element in all areas of so-called pastoral-tutorial work, and social education. The predisposition to learn is seen to be a question of social, cultural and emotional factors where all teaching places a necessary emphasis on the quality of relationships and the need for social and cognitive skills.

## CONCLUSION

The New Learning Initiative has attempted to embody these views of teaching and learning most explicitly in a specific cognitive education scheme, such as Instrumental Enrichment or the Oxfordshire Skills Programme, in school-community links activities and in residential education. IE is intended to provide the most direct experience of organising one's thinking and fundamental concept-forming processes, to be carried over into other areas of learning. This carry-over effect, or transfer, depends largely on similar methodology being used elsewhere so that all learning is problem-orientated. A short-cut to this end has been to provide pupils with very obviously 'active' and 'individuated' learning in the community and in residential situations, but it remains to be seen how far the curriculum as a whole, and our pedagogy, can become sufficiently flexible and negotiable to meet the needs of individual pupils no matter what their difficulties with learning.

## REFERENCES

Bruner, J. (1966) Towards a Theory of Instruction, Cambridge: Harvard University Press.

De Bono, E. (1970) Lateral Thinking: A Textbook of Creativity, Harmondsworth: Penguin.

________ (1973) CORT Thinking, Harmondsworth, Penguin.

________ (1976) Teaching Thinking, Harmondsworth, Penguin.

Feuerstein, R. (1979) Instrumental Enrichment, Baltimore: University Park Press.
Joseph, K. (1982) Text of a speech to CLEA conference.
Smith, R., Haywood, C. and Bransford, J. (1982) 'Assessing cognitive change; in McCauley, C. M., Sperber, R. and Brooks, P. (eds), Learning and Cognition in the Mentally Retarded, Hillsdale, New Jersey: Lawrence Erlbaum.

# 10 TEACHING APPROACHES AND STUDENT NEEDS

Nigel Collins

## INTRODUCTION

All pupils have needs and the needs of particular students are personal as well as special. Social backgrounds, maturation rates, interests, antipathies and learning styles are idiosyncratic. It is important, therefore, to avoid planning educational programmes on the assumption that some students have special needs and require special attention while others, the majority, are normal and can be dealt with summarily. This is not to deny that describable impairments and problematic behaviour patterns exist among students. Some of these, hearing impediments for example, are so common that schools can plan for them in advance. Schools will also have to contend with various kinds of persistent disruptive behaviour and may need to work out pre-emptive strategies for coping with them. The point is that the obvious special needs of some students should not blind schools to the special needs of all students. The most effective educational programmes will have built into them the capacity for assessing accurately the needs of all participants and attempting to meet them.

It should come as no surprise to find that the teaching and learning approaches which have this capacity for diagnosis and adaptation to individual needs are often those which are most appropriate for the student with obvious learning difficulties. What follows is a very brief discussion of some of these approaches and their implications for students and teachers with special reference to disaffected and disruptive students.

## ASSESSING NEEDS

A great deal of time and energy in schools goes into examining and testing students but how much goes into finding out what the student thinks about her or his own performance and future expectations? Yet a programme which aims to meet student needs with reference only to external observations and graded tests is going to miss the mark. If students are encouraged to discuss confidentially their own perceptions of their previous and anticipated learning, including their feelings about different teaching approaches, their ambitions, their worries about learning challenges and their enjoyment of learning experiences, there is some hope that teachers can begin to map out a learning route which will be motivating and beneficial to the individuals.

## LEARNING AGREEMENTS

The next step is to work towards a learning agreement with individual students which makes clear short- and longer-term learning objectives and the methods by which they will be achieved. Quite why so many secondary teachers react negatively to such an approach is difficult to understand when one considers the cost in time and effort of trying to carrying on regardless, against the pressures of entrenched or disruptive behaviour, with a prearranged standardised programme. We seem to be able to accept that the student in a wheelchair will need to agree an individualised programme, we sometimes accept that badly behaved students can only be taught if they agree their programme, but we rarely give the relatively able-bodied and well behaved students the chance to negotiate their learning. In this way we ensure that a number of students cross the threshold into one of the categories which qualifies them for special attention. Hence the usual fourth and fifth year indeterminate maladies and increasingly disruptive behaviour.

The teaching skills involved in assessing student needs and agreeing learning programmes include the ability to:

- communicate optimism about the student's capacity to reflect on her or his capabilities and plan for the future;

- elicit open statements about feelings and thoughts;
- 'read between the lines' when reticent, inarticulate, or belligerent students are making statements;
- set and review goals clearly.

## STUDENTS AS EDUCATIONAL RESOURCES

Negotiating learning programmes with students helps to ensure that the pace, the method and the content of the programmes are appropriate to that individual. It also uncovers unexpected enthusiasms and resources. How many student skills and interests are hidden from the sight of didactic teachers? Teachers who see themselves as sole importers of knowledge will only succeed with students who have been misled into thinking that they are solely absorbers of knowledge. Fortunately you cannot mislead all the students all the time and some will already refuse to accept this role. The fact is that learning is passing among students, irrespective of the teachers, all the time: learning about society, maturation, physical potential, relationships. Furthermore, this incidental learning is often felt by students to be more significant than the learning arranged by teachers. Students can and do teach each other and the wise teacher makes strategic use of this fact.

Not all students want to tell a teacher what they feel about learning programmes but will tell a friend. If that friend has been helped to give a response and is further involved in shaping and delivering subsequent learning there is a chance that the motivation of both students will be high. Student groups and classes, which are run on the principle of mutual support and corporate responsibility for the success of programmes, draw out significant strengths from their members and reach the individuals which teachers cannot reach.

## GROUP TUTORING

Group tutoring uses the interactions between students as an educational experience. Well organised group discussion or problem-solving is self-motivating: that is, the group is continually analysing what it is doing and how well it is responding to the task. Through this process many shy, diffident or antagonistic students can learn about their impact on the group and improve their performance, by experiment and imitation.

To run successful groupwork sessions teachers need some knowledge and experience of how people tend to behave in groups and a repertoire of tactics for intervening when groups are experiencing difficulty. But more important than this is the ability to maintain faith in the efficacy of groupwork even when sessions stumble or appear to be chaotic. If teachers lose nerve halfway through sessions or programmes and renege on agreements about group autonomy and cooperative approaches to problem-solving, they will seriously undermine the confidence of students and may not be able to create another opening for this type of learning approach. The key to successful groupwork is initial clarity in defining tasks and continuing confidence in the group's ability to overcome temporary setbacks.

## RELEVANCE

The emphasis on data processing in schools alienates large numbers of students who are not able to see the value of information which is unrelated to their immediate concerns. In order to be of service to these students, teaching programmes need to be able to demonstrate relevance. This means using examples drawn from local life, problem-solving which has a positive outcome for the student, environments like workplaces where the relevance of learning is manifest, and the experience and enthusiasms of the students. It also implies an emphasis on skills rather than the absorption of knowledge.

## FOCUS ON SKILLS

Disaffected students can be motivated by the prospect of skill acquisition. Most young people are keen to be seen as having a broad range of competence. If they can relate their efforts to useful outcomes even the most negative students can often be engaged. Furthermore, it is easier for students to assess their own progress in programmes which encourage them to put their learning into action. Since computers are so much faster and more accurate data processors, teachers would in any case be well advised to switch their emphasis away from information and towards skills, attitudes, beliefs and creative thinking.

All this is obviously more easily said than done. Very considerable teacher skills are implied: organisational skills, negotiating skills to open up learning possibilities in the communities or in firms, assignment design skills, and the capacity to run resource-led learning programmes. Teachers engaged in this kind of programme usually find they are learning as much as their students.

## ENVIRONMENTS

One of the reasons why many schools with theoretically enlightened teaching programmes do not succeed in engaging the enthusiasm and commitment of students is that they assume that these programmes should be run in school. School classrooms and laboratories are not always the best environment for learning to occur. Ask school-leavers what they particularly remember about their eleven years of compulsory schooling and you will discover that they talk mainly about field trips, work experience, residentials, visits, community service, street surveys, external conferences, weekend courses, foreign visits and camps.

In order to meet the needs of students we may have to ascertain the appropriate environment for a particular learning experience. If we did this thoroughly we might even discover that there were some things we currently teach which are best taught by others who have access to children in environments we cannot penetrate, such as the home. We might also have to accept that some truants who are illegally employed are learning more than we can teach them.

## INTEGRATED PASTORAL SUPPORT FOR STUDENTS

Teachers tend to offer to students a range of services which might be termed counselling and guidance. Some of these, like, for example, individual interviews to guide option choices, are part of the general curriculum offered to all students. Some are extra-curricular, for example, counselling for distressed students or disciplinary interviews.

It has already been suggested that counselling- type interviews should be an integral part of programme planning and review. What tends to happen, however, is that a division is created between student interviews which tackle factual, organisational or assessment issues and those which give attention to emotional, moral and behavioural issues. This division is unhelpful for a number of reasons. First, it ignores the fact that the two sets of issues are intimately related. Second, it encourages a discontinuity of pastoral support so that no member of staff has a rounded view of students. Third, it is likely to give the impression that emotional and moral support are available only for those able to demonstrate very urgent needs. Urgent needs are not the same as important needs. Such an impression will actually precipitate crises in some students who feel that this is the only way they can qualify for attention. The majority of students will keep quiet and receive no attention.

What is needed is an integrated system of pastoral support which makes all students feel that their various concerns are felt to be worthy of attention, and that they know to whom they should turn for this attention. In this way fewer students will 'play up' in order to get attention and there will be fewer instances of unhelpful categorisation of students.

## STUDENT RECORDING

If schools are helping their teachers to use negotiating counselling, group tutoring and skill-focused teaching skills, they have the basis upon which student recording, both formative and summative, can be based. Put the other way round, effective attention to the needs of students depends upon some kind of sharable and ongoing record of what is happening to the student as a learner and contributor to the learning of others. The actual process of keeping such a record up-to-date is in itself a valuable teaching tool since it can only be accurate if it involves matching the perception of tutor and student. Such matching requires careful dialogue, and raises the level of communication and evaluation skills in both teacher and student. In other words, teachers and students learn to talk to each other in a structured way against a background of decisions about what sort of experiences are considered to be relevant and what kind of criteria will be used to put a value on these experiences.

## CLIMATE BUILDING

In the training of primary teachers it is customary to focus attention on the creation of a positive learning environment. Trainees are encouraged to think about the physical conditions of their classrooms, the way they organise students into groups, the way they utilise learning materials, the way they encourage feedback, the style of their speech, the contingencies for difficult, diffident or distressed students and the way they will model the kind of learning attitude which they wish to foster in students.

In the training of secondary teachers several of these factors are given inadequate attention to the great detriment of the service to young people. The ambience created by teachers is as important as their knowledge of the subject. Indeed, since information can often be passed on relatively quickly once the student is receptive, a great deal of time should be spent attending to the climate in which the student is to learn. Experience has shown that people of all ages learn best if they feel safe, that is, protected from physical and psychological aggression, and if they are valued, that is, they are respected for what they are and what they can offer.

Schools and colleges which create a climate which fosters these feelings in students will get the best responses from them. The staff skills implied by such an endeavour are in the areas of maintaining positive and optimistic models of people, communicating with respect and without prejudice whatever the age, gender or race of the student, helping people to enhance their self-image, setting stimulating targets for performance and paying attention to the variety of formal and informal factors in the institution which might affect morale.

## STEREOTYPING AND PREJUDICE

If teachers truly want to meet the needs of students they are going to have to be rigorous about avoiding stereotyping. In recent years there has been increasing awareness of the fact that the student with very obvious needs, such as the mentally impaired person, is vulnerable to labelling and unhelpful special treatment. It is important to be respectful and unprejudiced with students whatever their race, gender or physical and mental attributes. This does not mean that teachers should treat everyone the same. It means that the starting point for teacher-student relationships should be unbiased mutual respect. If a student has obvious special needs such as the need to be helped to move or communicate, the teacher needs to be clear about the exact nature of the help required, sensitive to dignified ways of offering it and disciplined about not assuming the necessity for other kinds of special attention. The teacher is thus acting as the model for the whole group's attitude to, and treatment of the student.

In the case of students who frequently and deliberately disrupt classes, then teachers need to be just as scrupulous about avoiding prejudice. It is important to stick to the facts and gauge exactly what the student actually does without getting embroiled in generalisations about what sort of student he or she is. It is helpful to replace final judgements with open-ended observations which allow for change. Thus, instead of condemning a student for being 'violent' the teacher might observe that 'the student has yet to learn how to express feelings without inflicting harm on others'.

Dignity is a key word in dealing with disruptive students. Research has tended to show that such students rarely think highly of themselves. Insulting, humiliating and otherwise derogatory treatment of disruptive students is not only ethically unacceptable but counterproductive. The learning programmes which do most to help disruptive students are likely to be those which encourage these students to establish a sense of personal worth, help them to communicate feelings, give them a chance to practise social skills in a semi-safe environment and offer them good practice models of personal conduct.

## SUPPORTING AND DEVELOPING STAFF

The basic human needs of teachers and students are the same. A number of conditions have been mentioned which can contribute to an appropriate and effective service to students. Similar conditions, perhaps expressed in professional terms, will help to ensure that teachers perform well in the service of students.

Educational managers need to assess accurately the capabilities, potential and needs of their staff. They need to be clear about appropriate performance targets and will accordingly have to discuss and agree them with individual staff. Teachers, like students, need to be encouraged and helped to work together in teams towards common goals. Teachers will be motivated if they feel that they are engaged in activities which are relevant to these goals. The tasks set for teachers should predominantly involve using teaching skills rather than theorising about them. The environments in which teachers are asked to perform should be suitable for the task. The teaching profession should give teachers a feeling of being valued and adequately recompensed. The institutional conditions in schools and colleges should be dignified, resistant to prejudice, conducive to open communication and trust, and responsive to the ideas and feelings of staff. To help teachers in their work the school management must provide a structure within which teachers can evaluate their performance and rely on commitment to help them to improve and overcome difficulties. Finally, both students and staff should have access to someone who is able to listen to their concerns, help them work through personal problems and be prepared to act on their behalf in a crisis.

## SUMMARY

Effective learning programmes are designed around accurate assessment of the needs of individual students and the creation of a challenging but supportive learning environment in which students and staff agree to work together to achieve targets for personal development.

# 11 ABLE PUPILS IN OXFORDSHIRE SCHOOLS

Keith Postlethwaite, Mike Deans and Cliff Denton

## INTRODUCTION

More than half a century has passed since Terman carried out his now famous investigation of the characteristics of 1000 gifted pupils in America. Over this period, interest in the educational needs of this group of pupils in our schools has continued to develop. The first World Conference on Gifted Children took place in London in September 1975. This was followed two years later by the first United Kingdom national conference on this topic organised by the Department of Education and Science. Since then a growing number of LEAs have shown interest in the needs of the gifted and, in the past ten years, there has been a significant amount of curriculum development and research in the field. What is more, the pace of this development and research has been increasing.

In Oxfordshire, a study carried out at Banbury School in 1978 showed that able pupils who spent their first years in this comprehensive secondary school in mixed ability groups gained slightly better examination results than those who had spent their first years in streamed groups (Postlethwaite and Denton, 1978). This challenged simplistic notions that homogeneous ability grouping would provide a ready solution to the problems of able pupils in comprehensive schools, but offered no clear insights into how solutions might be developed. In this context the LEA set up an advisory panel for the gifted, drawing its membership from primary and secondary schools, advisory and support services, the LEA administration and Oxford University. At the same time the Oxford Educational Research Group (OERG) was established at the Oxford

University Department of Educational Studies (OUDES). This undertook a broad programme of research in, for example, modern languages, science and technology, and mathematics. It also directed attention to the issue of able pupils, beginning its work with a preliminary study funded by the Hulme Fund of Brasenose College. This revealed a wide interest amongst the teachers in the county in the education of able pupils, and led on to two large-scale research projects, both funded by the Department of Education and Science.

It is the purpose of this chapter to discuss some aspects of the curriculum development activities related to able pupils which have taken place in Oxfordshire, and to summarise some of the findings of the OERG research which has been carried out in this field.

## DEVELOPMENTS IN OXFORDSHIRE

Following the establishment of the advisory panel, a day conference for teachers was organised at Westminster College in 1981. This was attended by some 300 teachers and was addressed by Professor Ted Wragg, Dr Trevor Kerry and Graeme Clarke, among others. This added further stimulus to school-based activity within the county and led to several other successful, though at the time unrelated, activities. An important outcome was that the LEA subject advisers began to explore ways to enrich provision within their own specialist areas and were invited to discuss their plans with the advisory panel when they felt that it would be helpful to do so. There was also emphasis on the already well-established avenues for the pursuit of excellence in schools at area, county and national levels in competitive games and athletics; through the county service for instrumental teaching; through the successful Saturday Music Schools; through the County Youth Orchestra which, with independently performing sections, offered a challenge to young people and provided a chance to develop talents to the full as soloists or as contributors to group endeavours.

By this time, the Schools Science and Technology Centre was well established, allowing able pupils access to services and information within the University of Oxford. Other new initiatives were also taken. Staff of primary and secondary schools cooperated to organise music festivals, science fairs and activity days in the areas of the arts, languages, mathematics and movement. A group of teachers met together regularly over a two-year period to produce enrichment materials in humanities including material on the growth and development of Oxford. Teachers seconded from primary and middle schools became actively involved in a wide range of promotional work in schools, tackling areas such as problem-solving in science and Craft Design and Technology (CDT); running interest-based workshops; setting up links between schools and the local community so that pupils could tackle 'real' problems identified by local industry and business. Often these teachers worked closely with the OERG research staff who were also able to take part in some of the initiatives being developed in individual secondary schools - initiatives such as science-based problem-solving days for mixed age groups of pupils, which were set up by a school in close cooperation with local industry. Another development which was put into effect in several schools was the extension of the brief of special needs departments to take some responsibility for provision or coordination of provision for able pupils.

This range of activity encouraged OERG research staff, again working closely with seconded teachers and advisers, to hold two three-term DES Regional Courses through which teachers were encouraged to prepare materials and strategies to provide for able pupils in schools, and to adopt a critical attitude to the design and use of such materials.

By the middle of the academic year 1983/4, it was clear that there should be some central collection of materials that had been gathered from county and country-wide sources. In response, in January 1985 a Curriculum Enrichment Resources Centre was created as a focus for the coordination of provision for able pupils as part of the LEA's overall structure for pupils with special educational needs. The organisation of the centre was in the hands of one of the county special needs advisers, supported initially by a seconded teacher. The centre aims to provide a library of reference materials and has developed a catalogue of resources covering information, useful materials, details about supportive agencies and the names and interests of individuals willing to contribute expertise and enthusiasm.

A further significant development was the expression

of willingness, on the part of some 150 university dons, to work with groups of able pupils and with individuals. This offer too was supported by the Hulme Fund at Brasenose College, which provided resources to cover the costs of a coordinator, secretarial services, to reimburse dons visiting schools, and to subsidise centrally organised events such as day conferences in English, history, modern languages, mathematics and economics for sixth-form students. These conferences have become a regular feature of the local educational scene.

Thus much has been done, and is currently being done, in Oxfordshire, both to make appropriate provision for able pupils themselves, and to support teachers who are seeking to develop their own approaches to the education of such pupils. Concurrent with this activity on the part of teachers and the LEA, the DES-funded OERG research on able pupils, to which reference has already been made, was being conducted. This research was often closely associated with the LEA activity - both providing support for it, and gaining significant support from it. It is to the details of this research that we now turn.

## OERG RESEARCH ON ABLE PUPILS

The Oxford Educational Research Group has investigated the effectiveness of teacher-based identification of pupils who have high potential for performance in specific areas of the academic curriculum in secondary schools, and findings from this study will be discussed in some detail below. A later concern of the group was the effectiveness of enrichment materials as a form of provision for able pupils. It is not possible, at this stage, to give a detailed account of this part of the work, though we will refer very briefly to it below where we discuss how identification and provision might interrelate.

## EFFECTIVENESS OF TEACHER-BASED IDENTIFICATION

It is helpful to begin the discussion of this part of the research by setting out the relationship of the work, first to the broader definitions of giftedness which have found favour in recent years, and secondly to earlier studies of identification which have tended to concentrate on pupils with high IQ. The test-based method of identifying pupils with high subject-specific potential which was developed during the project, and which was used as the baseline against which to judge the effectiveness of teacher-based identification, will then be discussed. The extent of agreement between teacher-based and test-based identification will then be reported, and further insights into the process of teacher-based identification will be offered.

## DEFINITIONS

An important paper which discusses the identification of gifted pupils is that of Pegnato and Birch (1959). They chose a definition of giftedness which was based on the scores achieved by pupils on the Stanford-Binet IQ test, administered individually to pupils by an educational psychologist: pupils scoring 136 or more on this test were considered 'gifted'. In principle, working with such a definition, identification could be carried out with a high level of precision by individually testing all children in the schools. However, they point out that 'few schools [in the USA] have access to sufficient psychological services to provide for individual examination for all children' and therefore suggested that in practice identification should be carried out in two stages: first, the whole school population should be screened by means of group tests of IQ and of achievement. On this evidence appropriate pupils should be nominated for membership of a 'talent pool'. Second, these 'talent pool' pupils should be tested individually, by a psychologist, to determine which of them were indeed gifted. A similar procedure was recommended by Gallagher (1966) after his comprehensive survey of the research on identification which was then available.

In view of the definition of giftedness used by Pegnato and Birch, it is natural that they should have recommended individual testing by a psychologist as the second stage of their identification process. Their choice of group tests of IQ and achievement for the screening was based on two considerations. First, the screen must be effective to place in the talent pool all of those pupils who would have qualified for the label 'gifted' if everyone had been given the individual IQ test. Second, it should be as far as is possible efficient: it should minimise the number of 'non-gifted' who would also be placed in the talent pool. Pegnato and Birch considered the efficiency and effectiveness of several screening procedures. They showed that, used together, group tests of IQ and achievement were 97 per cent efficient and concluded that they provided the best means of screening. They also showed that, in the context of their study, teachers' nominations were neither effective nor efficient enough for them to be able to place much reliance on them for screening. They found teachers to be 45 per cent effective and 27 per cent efficient. Many other studies, using similar IQ-based definitions and following a similar methodology, have come to the same conclusion with regard to teacher nomination. Useful summaries of these are given by Jacobs (1971) and by Martinson (1975).

Some important work on approaches to provision for the gifted has made use of IQ-based definitions of giftedness (Bridges, 1969; Tempest, 1974; Bridges, 1975) and, of course, for such work the finding of the researches quoted above will be both pertinent and useful. However, there is considerable concern that these IQ-based definitions are unduly restrictive and that broader definitions of giftedness are needed. Powerful theoretical bases for such a view can be found in the multidimensional model of the intellect put forward by Guilford (1967). Admittedly the details of the model are disputed (Eysenck, 1967) and even Guilford admits that the model itself 'may or may not stand the test of time' (Guilford in Barbe and Renzulli, 1975). However, few would disagree with him when he goes on to express the view that the underlying principle of the 'multiplicity of intellectual abilities seems well established'. As a consequence of this theoretical position one is drawn towards the view of Greenberg (1955) who argues that IQ should be only one of a number of criteria used to define giftedness; and towards that of Torrance (1965) who stated that reliance on any single criterion is bound to lead us to overlook many extremely gifted individuals.

This case for broader definitions has been taken to heart by several LEAs in Britain. Reports from Devon County Council (1977) and from the City of Birmingham (1979) serve as useful examples of many LEA positions, and have had a great influence on definitions of giftedness in use in America. This can clearly be seen in a Report to

Congress made by the US Commissioner for Education (Marland, 1972), which refers to gifted children as children with high 'demonstrated achievement, and/or potential, in any of the following areas, singly or in combination: general intellectual ability, specific academic aptitude, creative or productive thinking, leadership ability, visual and performing arts, psychomotor activity'. The logic of such a broad definition is, of course, that methods of identification should be based on correspondingly broad principles. Renzulli and Smith (1977) have argued that to use an IQ test as the sole criterion to identify such children is 'questionable practice'. We would go further and suggest that to do so misses the point of the new definition completely.

This, of course, changes the perspective in which we should view the work of Pegnato and Birch, and of the other authors of similar studies. No longer should their findings and recommendations be seen as prescriptions for the identification of 'the gifted', but simply as recommendations for the identification of one sub-set of the gifted - a sub-set which is defined in terms of high IQ and which might be thought to approximate to Marland's (1972) group of children with 'high potential in the area of general intellectual ability'. To ignore their findings in relation to this sub-set is, of course, to act unwisely, but it is equally unwise to generalise these findings to other sub-sets without further study. Therefore, if understanding of identification is to be advanced we should seek to place, alongside these studies, other studies of the methods of identification appropriate to other sub-sets.

In the remainder of this chapter we will make a contribution to this process by discussing the identification of the sub-set with high 'specific academic aptitude'. This is a group of interest to teachers for several reasons. First, there can be little doubt that such pupils do have needs which are not always fully met by the normal routine of their schools. Evidence for this can be found in the work of Her Majesty's Inspectorate who make numerous references to such needs in their survey of secondary education (HMI, 1979). Second, it is important to note that the qualifications of the staff and the structure of the curriculum in secondary schools make it particularly possible to respond to the needs of these pupils - once, of course, they have been identified and the detailed nature of their needs has been explored. Despite the importance of this sub-set of gifted pupils, relatively little empirical guidance is available to help those who are responsible for identifying the appropriate pupils. It is for this reason that we chose to focus the OERG study on this sub-group of able pupils.

The OERG project was concerned with the identification of thirteen-year-old pupils who have potential for high future performance in one or more areas of the academic curriculum. Four areas were chosen for detailed study. These were English, French, physics and mathematics. In each of these subjects we were concerned with the relationship between test-based and teacher-based methods of screening the school population to identify a 'talent pool' - a group which we defined as consisting of that 10 per cent of pupils who, relative to their peers in their own school, have the potential for the highest future performance in that subject.

The choice of the fairly large proportion of 10 per cent for our talent pools in each subject reflects the concerns of HMI (1979) and others that far more than the top 2 per cent who are traditionally regarded as 'gifted' have need of some, perhaps fairly limited, additional or alternative provision. The decision to define the group relative to their peers in their own school was taken as the needs of particular children will clearly be dependent upon the context in which they are educated. This point was discussed at some length, and a similar conclusion was reached, in the report of the City of Birmingham study group which was referred to earlier (City of Birmingham, 1979).

Before proceeding with the study of the two screening procedures it was necessary to agree upon measures of 'future performance' to which the study could relate. It was decided that this measure should be O-level performance in the given subject. Several reasons lay behind this choice. First, the 10 per cent target groups for this study lay well within the band for which the O-level examinations are designed. Second, evidence suggests that O-level performance in a subject is highly correlated with later performance at A-level in that subject.

This line of argument can be continued, though with admittedly attenuated force, by noting that A-level has been found to be an important factor in predicting degree success, particularly for science students (Entwistle and Wilson, 1977). Third, in the absence of other widely used and reliable tests of subject specific performance, it is difficult to identify any practicable alternative measure.

Having chosen this measure of 'future performance', the next task was to produce some test-based measures, which could be used with thirteen-year-old pupils as an indicator of their potential for performance at O-level in each of the four subjects. This was done by giving a number of tests to third-year pupils in two comprehensive schools and then following these pupils through to their O-level examinations. The tests which the pupils took were mainly from the Differential Aptitude Test battery (Bennett et al., 1974). Multiple regression analysis was then used to find, for each subject, a prediction equation which could be used to generate, from a pupil's test scores at 13+, a predicted O-level score for that pupil. These predicted O-level scores in a subject were then interpreted as a measure of the pupil's potential for performance in that subject.

Having thus established some useful test-based measures of potential, they were applied to new groups of thirteen-year-old pupils in eleven comprehensive schools. In each school, and in each subject, it was then a simple matter to draw up a list of pupils in order of their measured potential. However, care had to be exercised in interpreting these lists. The test-based measure of potential is not without error. The effect of this error is that a large group of pupils with the same predicted O-level score cannot all be expected to get exactly that score on their actual O-level. In fact, the actual O-level scores of the members of such a group will normally be distributed about their predicted score with a mean equal to the predicted score and a standard deviation equal to the standard error of the prediction. Thus some pupils' potential will have been underestimated by the test measure, and some overestimated. The magnitude of the error is such that it would be difficult to rely exclusively on the tests to determine the actual potential of any one individual pupil. However, if care is taken to take account of the error, the test-based measure of potential can be used to shed light on the validity of other screening methods. We now describe how the tests were used in this role.

First, in each subject, in each school, the top 10 per cent of pupils on the appropriate rank ordered list were identified as Group 1. These pupils were those who, on the evidence of the tests alone, had the best chance of being in the top 10 per cent on their actual O-level performance two and a half years later. A second group, Group 2, consisted of pupils whose scores were a little below the lowest score in Group 1, but were close enough to this lowest score so that, in view of the error associated with the test, they could be said to have at least a one-in-four chance of being in the top 10 per cent on their actual O-level score. Group 3 consisted of the rest of the pupils. Even taking test error into account, these pupils had at most a one-in-four chance of being in the top 10 per cent on actual O-level score - most of them, far down the list, had much less than this one-in-four chance. Thus, on the test evidence alone, Group 1 represented the pupils most likely to be in the top 10 per cent on actual O-level score; Group 2 those who had a reasonable chance of being in the top 10 per cent on actual O-level score; and Group 3 those who were unlikely to be in the top 10 per cent on actual O-level score.

Teachers in each subject in each school were also asked to nominate pupils for the 'top 10 per cent' talent pool and the details of the specification of this talent pool were discussed with them. Comparisons of these teacher-based nominations with pupils' test scores enabled us to assess the effectiveness of teacher-based identification. Further investigation, based on teacher interviews, or personal construct methodology and on a study of the use of checklists, gave some insights into the process of teacher-based identification.

## RESULTS OF THE EFFECTIVENESS OF TEACHER-BASED IDENTIFICATION

In English, 61 per cent of the pupils whom teachers nominated for the talent pool were in Group 1 on the basis of the test results. That is, these pupils would also have been nominated if screening had been based entirely on pupils' predicted O-level performance as measured by the tests. A further 25 per cent of teachers' nominations were of pupils in group 2, those who, on the evidence of the tests, had at least a one-in-four chance of being in the top 10 per cent on actual O-level performance. Because of the uncertainty introduced as a result of the test error, we can conclude that, on the evidence of the tests, there is little reason to question the appropriateness of the 86 per cent of teacher nominations which have been discussed above. However, the remaining 14 per cent of teacher nominations were of pupils who, according to the tests, had only a small chance of being in the top 10 per cent on actual O-based performance. We cannot be certain that teachers would nominate these pupils, but the test scores of these pupils do give cause for some concern. The situation in mathematics was identical to that in English. In French and physics the figures were rather less encouraging but still indicated that 69 per cent of teacher nominations were, in test terms, pupils with a good chance of being in the top 10 per cent on actual O-level score. The lists of pupils who had been identified by teachers were also inspected to assess how often children who were in the 'top 2 per cent' in terms of test results were included.

In English, French and mathematics, though to a lesser degree in physics, most pupils who might, on the basis of the test, be regarded as having very high ability in a subject were actually included in the teachers' 'top 10 per cent' group in that subject. Interestingly, in all subjects, many more of these pupils were overlooked by teachers when they were asked to indicate which pupils they thought were in 'top 5 per cent' groups.

These results suggest, therefore, that teachers' nominations for the 'top 10 per cent' were, especially in English and mathematics, largely confirmed by the test results. This is a somewhat different conclusion from that of researchers such as Pegnato and Birch. We were, of course, looking at a rather different target group and might, therefore, have expected somewhat different results. It is useful, however, to attempt to explain the discrepancy between the two sets of findings in a little more detail.

First, there were some methodological problems inherent in the earlier studies. Perhaps the most significant was that no discussion was entered into between the researchers and the teachers about the definition of the target group for which teachers were asked to nominate pupils. As a consequence, it may be that teachers were simply operating on a dimension which was different from that of the tests that were, in effect, being used to validate their nominations. The resulting mismatch between teacher and test may have been as much an outcome of this different interpretation of what was meant by 'gifted', as a result of the teachers' inability to identify correctly the pupils who fell within the definition which they were themselves using. Questions of definition and identification were therefore confused.

Second, there was no attempt to take account of test error in the earlier studies. This is bound to increase the extent of the error ascribed to the other screening processes, such as teacher judgement, that were studied.

Finally, one should bear in mind that the assessment of overall intelligence is a rather artificial task for a secondary school teacher. Teacher and pupil work together on a specific subject, and the nature of the tasks undertaken is therefore limited. The kinds of information available to the teacher could therefore be expected to be more relevant to the task of identifying pupils for the target groups with which we have been concerned, than to the identification of pupils for the target group in which Pegnato and Birch, for example, were interested. Research reviewed by Cook (1979) confirms the commonsense view that judgements are likely to be more accurate where relevant information is available to those making them.

## INSIGHTS AND TEACHER-BASED IDENTIFICATION

Further investigation of teacher-based identification was undertaken to try to gain more insight into how teachers identified able pupils, what might be leading to the somewhat less effective levels of identification in French and physics, and what might be done to help teachers, especially of these two subjects, to be more effective.

The study of how teachers identified pupils was done in three ways. First, teachers' nominations were compared with pupils' scores on creativity and attitude tests; then, with their social class and gender, a score for the neatness of their work, and with their results on the individual sub-scales of the Differential Aptitude Test Battery. This measured such things as verbal ability, numerical ability, mechanical reasoning, clerical speed and accuracy. In this way we were able to see which individual aptitudes were associated with being identified as able by a teacher.

Second, teachers were interviewed about pupils whom they had selected, and about able pupils, in terms of the test, whom they had overlooked. Third, a personal construct study was conducted with teachers to refine insights from these open-ended interviews.

The test-based study of the characteristics of pupils who were identified by teachers suggested that, despite some variation from school to school, there were some characteristics that were consistently associated with teacher-based identification in a given subject. The study also revealed that there was variation in the nature of these characteristics from subject to subject.

In English, for example, the variable most often highly correlated with teacher-based selection was language usage. In six schools correlations exceeded 0.5. No other variable was so highly correlated with teacher-based identification in English in schools. In physics, however, the variable most often highly correlated with teacher-based selection was general ability. In five schools this correlation exceeded 0.5. No other variable was highly correlated with teacher-based selection in physics in schools. These findings were consistent with the fact that English teachers were more effective than physics teachers in identifying able pupils, for language usage was the aptitude most highly correlated with O-level performance in English whereas mechanical reasoning, not general ability, was the aptitude most highly correlated with performance in physics.

Social class and neatness were not usually characteristics of teacher-selected pupils, once the effect of the correlations between these and other variables had been allowed for. Only in French did a noticeable number (five) of the teachers in individual schools show a bias towards pupils of a particular sex. This was consistently in favour of the selection of girls.

There was some indication that teacher-based selection was associated with favourable attitude scores, especially in French and physics. The open-ended interviews with teachers about individual pupils produced results that were entirely consistent with these findings from the test-based study.

The personal construct study also provided confirmatory evidence. Teachers of English were shown to be more sensitive to detailed subject-specific aspects of ability than were their colleagues in other subjects. Also, teachers of physics and French offered more attitudinal constructs than did English and mathematics teachers. A more detailed analysis of the personal construct data in physics revealed that these attitudinal constructs may often have acted as favouring or disqualifying cues for the teachers - pupils with favourable attitudes being identified despite contradictory evidence of other kinds, and pupils with poor attitudes being overlooked despite other evidence that they were of high ability.

In an attempt to discover what might be done to help teachers, especially French and physics teachers, to be more effective in identifying able pupils we designed a subject-specific checklist for each subject and compared the effectiveness of teachers who used these instruments with that of teachers who did not.

In the first year of the research, teachers in half the schools were asked to use a subject-specific checklist to guide them in making a second round of identification, roughly one term after their first, unguided attempt. The checklists were handed out to the teachers who were expected to do the exercise in a relatively short time (two weeks). There was no evidence that the checklists, used in this way, improved the accuracy of teacher-based identification in any subject.

In the second year teachers in English, French and physics were asked to use essentially the same checklists, but to fill them in over a period of a term or more. Used in this way the English and French checklists still produced no significant effect. In physics, however, there was a significant difference between checklist users and non-users, with users being accurate in their identifications. This suggested that, when used over a significant period of time, checklists can be but will not necessarily be useful. A cautious, investigatory approach to checklist use is therefore recommended.

In mathematics, a classroom observation study was conducted so that a researcher could study the problems of checklist use at first hand. It was found that an observer in the classroom could see, and record, more information about individual pupils' mathematical abilities than could their teacher; that even the observer could not see evidence of pupils' performance across the whole range of checklist items because some abilities were not being exercised by the work being done with the class; that a fuller picture could be obtained if the observer actively questioned pupils to diagnose their level of ability on particular checklist items; that study of pupils' normal workbooks revealed few clues relevant to checklist completion. These findings suggest reasons for the limited success of checklists in other subjects and could be interpreted as indicating ways in which checklists might, more effectively, be used.

## RELATIONSHIP BETWEEN IDENTIFICATION AND PROVISION

Having presented some background to the OERG research, and set out some of the results and related them to the findings in earlier studies, we now turn to some suggestions for a scheme of identification to which we have been drawn in the course of our work. We suggest that, if one is interested in making additional or alternative provision for those with high potential for achievement in a particular subject, one might begin by using teacher nomination to identify a top 10 per cent. We have shown that teacher-based identification of this broad target group is effective in English and mathematics, that it is reasonably effective in French and physics, that, at least in physics, sensitive use of subject-specific checklists can be helpful, and that in all subjects pupils in particular need of extensive additional provision - the top 2 per cent, say - are likely to be included in this group. If some fairly limited provision is then made for the whole of this group by the use of enrichment materials, some benefits can be expected; for although one OERG project on provision showed that management of such materials was not without problems for teachers, we also demonstrated that some, albeit quite small, increases in pupils' subject-specific performance could be detected.

Furthermore, the way in which individual pupils deal with the concepts and the techniques required of them by this provision might well provide the teacher with useful clues to enable a more accurate identification of the top 2 per cent to be made. If then, further provision for the 2 per cent, perhaps by means of acceleration, tutorial teaching or summer school attendance, was felt to be desirable, it would be easier for teachers to identify the appropriate pupils with confidence. It would seem that test results need not be an essential component of such a system, though, by alerting teachers to individuals about whom test and teacher disagreed, they may encourage teachers to take a second look at the pupils who for one reason or another might be difficult to assess correctly. An interesting upward spiral could be involved here.

The teachers' involvement in such programmes of provision for the 10 per cent and 2 per cent groups could well alert them to more things which characterise the work of able children and could, as a result, improve their ability to screen the next year's intake with even greater accuracy. There is also, of course, a valuable outcome for the able pupils. In such a scheme all pupils in the top 10 per cent talent pool would get some benefit from the provision made for them. In screening systems based on testing alone, there is a risk that all they would get is an individual IQ test.

There is, also, an interesting implication in these suggestions, for those who seek to make some central provision for the most able 1 to 2 per cent from a number of schools. If teachers are to be asked to nominate the pupils for such provision, as they frequently are, this nomination is likely to be more accurate if the individual schools are also engaged in making some provision for a broader group. Teacher nomination of the top 2 per cent in isolation from any such school-based provision is, by extrapolation from our findings discussed above, likely to overlook significant proportions of the target group children.

## FUTURE DEVELOPMENTS

From what has been said above, it is clear that much is being done in Oxfordshire. What is more, many of the activities which have been described are in the process of further development. Discussions are taking place, for example, to find ways in which the offer of help from university teachers can be taken up in the service of younger children than have, to date, benefited from it. There are also new initiatives to be taken, for example, to find ways in which more flexible secondary school timetabling, including the adoption of modular timetable structures, can be used to facilitate provision for able pupils as well as all others in the school, and to capitalise on national educational developments which could enable teachers to build provision for the able into their mainstream work. A good example would be GCSE, with its emphasis on differentiation of teaching and assessment, and with its reference to the development of pupils' ability to handle the processes of a subject as well as to acquire the appropriate knowledge of facts and concepts. Finally, we would suggest that research findings are now available which can continue to inform practice and encourage its development. We suggest that 'gifted education' in the county is still an important growth point which could improve the outcomes of education for this particular group of pupils and, at the same time, give valuable insights into how to cater properly for the whole range of ability and disability in our classes.

## REFERENCES


Barbe, W.B. and Renzulli, J.S. (1975) *Psychology and Education of the Gifted*, 2nd edn, New York: Irvington.

Bennett, G.K., Seashore, H.G. and Wesman, A.G. (1974) *5th Manual for the Differential Aptitude Tests*, New York: Psychological Corporation.

Bridges, S.A. (1969) *Gifted Children and the Brentwood Experiment*, London: Pitman.

—— (1975) *Gifted Chidren and the Millfield Experiment*, London: Pitman.

City of Birmingham Education Committee (1979) *Gifted and Outstanding Children*, Birmingham: LEA.

Cook, M. (1979) *Perceiving Others*, London: Methuen.

Devon County Council (1977) *Find the Gifted Child*, Devon Education Department.

Entwistle, N. and Wilson, J. (1977) *Degrees of Excellence*, London: Hodder and Stoughton.

Eysenck, H.J. 'Intelligence assessment', *Brit. J. Educ. Psychol.*, 37.

Gallagher, J.J. (1966) *Research Summary on Gifted Child Education*, Illinois: Department of Programme Development for Gifted Children.

Greenberg, L. (1955) 'Critique of classic methods of identifying gifted children', *School Rev.*, 63.

Guilford, J.P. (1967) *The Nature of Human Intelligence*, New York: McGraw Hill.

HMI (1979) *Aspects of Secondary Education*, London: HMSO.

Jacobs, J.C. (1971) 'Effectiveness of teacher and parent identification of gifted children as a function of

school level', Psychology in the Schools, 8. pp. 140-2.
Marland, S.P. (1972) Education of the Gifted and Talented, Report to Congress by the US Commissioner for Education, vol. 1, Washington DC.
Martinson, R.A. (1975) The Identification of the Gifted and Talented, Virginia: Council for Exceptional Children.
Pegnato, C.W. and Birch, J.W. (1959) 'Locating gifted children in high schools: a comparison of methods'. Exceptional Children, 25.
Postlethwaite, K. and Denton, C. (1978) Streams for the Future, Banbury: Pubansco Press.
Renzulli, J. and Smith, L.H. (1977) 'Two approaches to the identification of gifted students', Exceptional Children, 43, pp. 512-18.
Tempest, N.R. (1974) Teaching Clever Children 7-11, London: Routledge & Kegan Paul.
Torrance, E.P. (1965) Gifted Child in the Classroom, New York: MacMillan.

# PART 4: IN-SERVICE TRAINING, MICROELECTRONICS, THE COMMUNITY

# 12 IN-SERVICE EDUCATION AND SPECIAL NEEDS

Frank Hodgson and Alan Trotter

## INTRODUCTION

The field of special education currently represents a major area of change within the education system, the pressure for change resulting in the setting up of the Warnock Committee followed by legislation in the form of the 1981 Education Act.

The new special education legislation has caused schools to reappraise the arrangements they make for meeting pupils' special educational needs with a view to increasing their capacity to respond to the needs of a wider range of pupils. Increasingly, mainstream teachers are coming to realise that learning difficulties are the result of a mismatch between pupil performance and curricular demands rather than being caused by within-child deficits. Booth (1985), commenting on mainstream provision, makes the point that:

> the number of pupils with special needs is not seen as a fixed quantity of the school population but reflects the success with which schools adapt curricula to a diversity of abilities, backgrounds, interests and needs.

Clearly, if an existing curriculum is to be matched to the aptitudes, interests and needs of individual pupils, ways of working have to be explored which encourage the sharing of expertise between special education specialists and subject specialists. Bowers (1984) suggests that the skills to be shared between colleagues might include:

- the assessment of individual pupils;
- curriculum development and modification;
- devising appropriate learning programmes;
- adaptation and development of materials and technology;
- co-teaching skills.

As well as encouraging closer cooperation between teacher colleagues, the new legislation also demands effective working relationships with parents, and a range of professionals to provide support for the child, his family and his school. Circular 1/83, which considers the implications of the 1981 Education Act and the Education (Special Educational Needs) Regulations 1983 for the assessment and statements of special educational needs, declares in paragraph 6:

> Assessment should be seen as a partnership between teachers, other professionals, and parents, in a joint endeavour to discover and understand the nature of the difficulties and needs of individual children.

It is recommended in paragraph 8 that the LEA guidelines to schools on the arrangements for identifying, assessing and meeting special educational needs should relate to the identification and assessment procedures, channels of communication for referrals, and specialist services available for referrals. It advises, in paragraph 9, that the guidelines:

> should allow for the progressive extension of professional involvement from the class teacher to the headteacher, a specialist teacher, the educational psychologist, the school doctor and nurse, and other professionals in the education, health and social services. The child's parent should be involved and kept fully informed at every stage.

For teachers to develop more effective strategies for working with pupils with special educational needs and the above range of concerned adults, their professional development needs to be enhanced to improve their competence for meeting the needs of such pupils. This is acknowledged in Circular 1/83 when it is stated in paragraph 11 that it is expected that local education authorities will encourage INSET to assist teachers in recognising and meeting special educational needs.

For all the importance attached to INSET in the process of educational change, concern has been expressed quite widely as to its effectiveness. This includes concern by the government itself (DES, 1985), where it is recognised that the annual expenditure on INSET is not being used to best advantage, on the grounds that:

> a much more systematic approach is needed to the planning of inservice training at school and LEA level, which would seek to match training both to the career needs of teachers and to desired curricular changes in school.

It has been declared that legislation to extend the Secretary of State's power to grant-aid INSET is the means to achieve this aim. Circular 6/86 describes the LEA Training Grants Scheme, introduced on 1 April 1987, to improve the quality of teaching and further the professional development of teachers through support for local authorities in the training of teachers.

One of the nine national priority areas at schools level included in the scheme is training to meet the special educational needs of pupils with learning difficulties. The intention is that all INSET supported through the scheme should be monitored by the LEAs to assess the impact of a more effective and efficient delivery of the education service; an important inclusion bearing in mind previous accounts of the relative ineffectiveness of INSET programmes.

Henderson and Perry (1981) put forward two main reasons for the ineffectiveness of INSET programmes:

- a mismatch between the needs of teachers and course content;
- course participants being unable to use their newly acquired skills and knowledge because they were unable to influence what was happening in their schools.

An absence of follow-up support is cited by Fullan (1982) as the biggest single problem in professional development, claiming that higher education institutions are not set up to contribute to the kind of professional development which requires a continuing relationship with schools and LEAs.

Dalin (1978) in an examination of the limits to educational change, formed the opinion that many innovative programmes had failed because the innovators had a basically 'content orientation', taking for granted strategies of educational change. He traced much of the lack of success back to an inadequate understanding of schools as organisations, the process of change and the management of change.

Until relatively recent times the vast majority of INSET programmes have focused on the professional development of individual teachers, mainly through externally provided courses. More recent initiatives have adopted a change in focus to the school as the unit of change with the development of school-focused programmes. School-focused programmes were a frequent response to the quest for more effective ways of improving teachers and schools undertaken by CERI (1982) for the OECD. Throughout the conferences, seminars and reports, there was a recurring plea for INSET:

- to be rooted in practice;
- to be relevant;
- to be context-specific;
- to base its theory upon an analysis of practice.

For school-focused INSET to be effective, CERI stressed, a sound, well-integrated external support structure is required.

Hopkins (1986), addressing the issue of INSET and educational development, feels that when INSET programmes are developed from a school's identified needs, not only is the mismatch between teacher need and course context avoided, but the probability of implementation is increased with the involvement of the staff in programme planning. Account can be taken of constraints imposed by resources known to be available to the school.

In support of educational change being institutionally focused rather than teacher focused, Eraut (1972) describes a three-component model for institutional innovation:

- a mechanism for institutional self-evaluation and the identification of institutional problems;
- provision of resources (not restricted to equipment/ materials, but including teacher planning time, release for INSET etc) for development work aimed at solving institutional problems;
- consultancy support.

Guidelines have been published by the DES (1978) for increasing the effectiveness of INSET, indicating the following practical steps to be taken by a school in the planning of an appropriate programme to respond to identified needs:

- identify INSET needs of:
  - individual teachers
  - functional groups of teachers
  - the school as a whole;
- decide which needs should have priority, then implement appropriate INSET programme;
- evaluate effectiveness of programme;
- practical use to be made of knowledge and skills gained.

The flexibility of the GRIST funding arrangements encourages the development of a variety of INSET opportunities to support school-focused initiatives. Traditional award-bearing courses can be augmented by different forms of INSET activities, such as:

- self-study, supported by distance learning;
- school/LEA based working groups;
- consultancy support;
- visits;
- teacher fellowships.

Where appropriate, successful participation in the above activities could accumulate credits towards a recognised qualification as part of a modular INSET programme of the type described by Robson (1984).

Under the new special education legislation, teachers with responsibilities for pupils with special needs, and other senior staff, are expected to carry out a wider range of management functions associated with a whole school approach to meeting special educational needs. To be in a position to make a positive response to changing arrangements, these senior members of staff will need:

- to update their knowledge of current policies and practices in the field of special education;
- to increase their competence in the interpersonal skills for working with the pupils, their parents, teacher colleagues and other professionals.

We contend that if in-service courses are to be effective in helping teachers to manage the provision of education for learners with special needs, it is not appropriate simply to run INSET as a single package, requiring teachers to attend for a taught programme in the providing institution. There need to be three interconnected phases involving several parties to support the participating teacher.

## PHASE ONE: SITUATIONAL ANALYSIS AND COMMITMENT

The institution providing INSET, the LEA, and the schools should together carry out a situational analysis of the nature of the problems and challenges in each of the schools participating in the INSET course. During this process each school should nominate the key staff who have to manage the tasks relating to special needs provision. These individuals should be asked to prioritise and specify the concrete goals for the school and agree - in consultation with the INSET providers - to bring these to the in-service course as projects. Equally, the senior management of the school should make a commitment to support the progress of the project and to the implementation of its solution/recommendations after the INSET course.

## PHASE TWO: THE IN-SERVICE COURSE PROGRAMME

Whether as a full-time or part-time programme the course should cater for the following:

### Action learning projects

This would be a process in which course participants work

on their identified goals and tasks with a view to preparing a strategy for implementation in their respective schools. If the course were a part-time programme of long duration the implementation might be started during the INSET programme; if it were a full-time course the implementation would begin after the course. It would be tempting for INSET staff to want to help participants towards these goals through conventional tutorials; but the process could be more effective if, in addition, staff convinced participants that as well as learning for themselves, they could also learn with and from each other. This approach to engage in Action Learning (Revans, 1980, 1984) recognises that people who face real problems can become 'partners in adversity', and are more likely to produce feasible solutions to actual problems than if they rely solely on the support of academic staff who, whatever their past experience and present expertise, do not themselves own the problems. This is not to deny the value of such staff but rather - as will be shown below - to suggest that they can make a distinct contribution in other ways.

## Developing relevant knowledge and skills

There should be a programme of content which is both useful in itself and is also applicable to the action learning projects. The areas included should satisfy three criteria: topics which all teachers concerned with special needs have to be competent in; topics which are identified by the totality of the situational analyses carried out in the participating schools; and, topics which will assist and enhance the action learning process. Therefore the areas covered will vary according to the composition of the participants and their schools. It will be the distinct task of the staff providing INSET to diagnose, negotiate and get this programme right. Notwithstanding this negotiated process, it is possible to envisage the inclusion of the following content areas to meet these criteria:

### Implications of new legislation for mainstream SEN practice

For pupils with special educational needs to have access to a school's range of curricular opportunities, and to share in these activities with other pupils, consideration needs to be given to issues such as:

- school and classroom organisation;
- resource allocation;
- curriculum modification;
- monitoring pupil progress;
- parental participation in their child's educational progress;
- parental rights in the assessment procedures;
- development of staff support teams, including support from outside the school.

Self-management

This could be included for its benefit to any educationalist carrying out management roles. It is not a subject that features in most INSET courses, but is being given increasing emphasis in general Management Development Programmes (Pedler and Boydell, 1985). In addition, this topic can include the ways in which teachers can cope with stress, a phenomenon increasingly apparent in education (Dunham, 1986).

Problem-solving strategies

This is a subject which teachers could usefully consider in relation to the management of education as distinct from problem-solving for intellectual learning purposes. The benefits would be the applicability of problem-solving models to the goals/tasks brought to the course by participants and worked at in action learning. There are several ways in which the subject could be approached. Two effective approaches are found in Taylor (1985) and Jackson (1985).

### Managing and communicating

The first part of this chapter indicated the need for those responsible for special educational needs to work together with parents, and other teachers as professionals. To establish, manage and sustain cooperation with these parties, in order to design curricular structures and to harmonise educational expertise for the benefit of the children concerned, will call for a repertoire of skills in: leadership, planning, organisation (Havelock, 1973;

Paisey, 1981; Adair, 1983; De Bono, 1983; Handy and Aitken, 1986; Hoyle, 1986); team building (Belbin, 1981; Collins, 1986); communication counselling (Bolton, 1979; Nelson-Jones, 1986); negotiation (Collins, 1986); and conflict resolution (Likert, 1976; De Bono, 1985). These can be developed on two fronts.

First, through insights derived from the literature it would be the responsibility of INSET staff to make apt selections from both educational and more general management literature for the consideration of participants. The sources suggested above have been found useful. Second, to give structured practice in these skills to simulate in non-threatening situations the ways in which these skills would have to be applied in real professional work. Of course, the selection and priority of these topics would be negotiable with the group of participants, and the coverage and balance would be constrained by the time available. Equally, there could be other topics identified by participants which could also be included. At all events the intention in Phase Two would be to help participants to learn about the management of people and change and would be directed towards the construction of strategies and solutions for the real problems which teachers had brought to the course. By the end of Phase Two, involving attendance at the INSET course centre, each course member should have produced a plan to implement. Teachers would have produced this by a combination of individual study, tutorials, action learning, new knowledge, skill development, and - depending on the structure of the course - one or more visits back to their school to brief senior management and colleagues on the progress and emerging proposals. Ideally, the headteacher should also visit the course to take part in a seminar together with staff, action learning participants and LEA representatives to hear and discuss what his member of staff had proposed.

## PHASE THREE: IMPLEMENTING THE STRATEGIES

Normally, an in-service course would end after Phase Two. However, in the model suggested here, it would continue in a different location. The locus of control would now be exercised by the participant and the supporting staff in the teacher's own school. It would be their responsibility to implement the solutions arrived at during Phase Two. Staff of the institution providing the INSET course would visit the school(s) concerned to assist in clarification and implementation. Ideally, other members of the action learning group would also visit to lend support. All of these efforts would be directed towards helping to overcome the difficulties which staff returning from INSET courses typically have in bringing about real change. Finally, if possible, there should be a day or session after the course in which former participants return to the INSET centre to report and discuss the new problems which they have encountered during implementation, and consider the next steps to achieve desired outcomes.

## REFERENCES

Adair, J. (1983) Effective Leadership, London: Pan.

Belbin, R.M. (1981) Management Teams, London: Heinemann.

Bolton, R. (1979) People Skills, London: Prentice Hall.

Booth, T. (1985) 'In-service training and progress in special education', in Sayer, J. and Jones N. (eds), Teacher Training and Special Educational Needs, Beckenham: Croom Helm.

Bowers, A. (1984) 'Change in the special school', in Bowers, A. (ed.), Management and the Special School, Beckenham: Croom Helm.

CERI (1982) In-Service Training and Training of Teachers: A Condition of Educational Change, Paris: OECD.

Collins, N. (1986) New Teaching Skills, Oxford: Blackwell.

Dalin, P. (1978) Limits to Educational Change, London: Macmillan.

De Bono, E. (1983) Atlas of Management Thinking, Harmondsworth: Penguin.

——— (1985) Conflicts, Harmondsworth: Penguin.

Department of Education and Science (1978) Making INSET Work, London: HMSO.

——— (1981) Education Act 1981, London: HMSO.

——— (1983) Circular 1/83, Assessments and Statements of Special Educational Needs, London: HMSO.

_____ (1985) White Paper: Better Schools, London: HMSO.

_____ (1986) Circular 6/86: Local Education Authority Training Grant Scheme, HMSO.

Durham, J. (1986) Stress in Teaching, Beckenham: Croom Helm.

Eraut, M. (1972) In-Service Education for Innovation, NCET Occasional Paper, 4.

Fullan, M. (1982) The Meaning of Educational Change, Ontario: OISE Press.

Handy, C. and Aitken, R. (1986) Understanding Schools as Organisations, Harmondsworth: Penguin.

Harland, M. (ed.) (1986) School Management Skills, London: Heinemann.

Havelock, R.G. (1973) The Change Agent's Guide to Innovation in Education, New York: Englewood Cliffs.

Henderson, E. and Perry, S. (1981) 'School-focused INSET evaluation', Cambridge Journal of Education, Vol. 9.

Hopkins, D. (1986) In-Service Training and Educational Development, Beckenham: Croom Helm.

Hoyle, E. (1986) The Politics of School Management, London: Hodder and Stoughton.

Jackson, K. (1985) The Art of Problem Solving, Reading: Comino Foundation, Bulmershe College.

Likert, R. and J. G. (1976) New Ways of Managing Conflict, New York: McGraw Hill.

Nelson-Jones, R. (1986) Human Relationship Skills, London: Holt, Rinehart and Winston.

Paisey, A. (1981) Organisation and Management in Schools, London: Longman.

Pedler, M. and Boydell, T. (1985) Managing Yourself, London: Fontana.

Revans, R.W. (1980) Action Learning, London: Blond and Briggs.

_____ (1984) The Sequence of Managerial Achievement, Bradford: MCB.

Robson, C. (1984) 'A modular in-service advanced qualification for teachers of children with special needs', British Journal of In-Service Education 11, pp. 32-36.

Taylor, M. (1985) Getting Things Done, Further Education Unit, Department of Education and Science, London: HMSO.

# 13 MICROTECHNOLOGY AND THE ASSESSMENT OF COMMUNICATION DIFFICULTIES

Pru Fuller and Tim Southgate

## INTRODUCTION

Microtechnology can enormously enhance the learning opportunities of children with communication difficulties. This chapter describes the work of the ACE Centre which was established to provide information and advice about the use of microelectronic aids to communication in education. In particular, the importance of a multi-professional approach to the assessment of children's communication needs is discussed.

The ability to communicate is vital to the health and development of all individuals. Not only do we need to make known our more basic needs, we must exchange information with those around us and express our emotions. Without effective communication, the opportunity to interact with others, to exercise control over our environment and to develop intellectually, socially and emotionally is restricted. The life of a person without effective communication may be uncomfortable and hazardous and marked by isolation and frustration.

A factor common to many children with special needs is that the ability to communicate is in some way impaired. Sometimes, the effects of communication impairment may be immediately apparent. A child with a severe physical disability may be unable to write or to speak, to hold a book or turn its pages. A visually impaired child may be unable to read normally and a child who is profoundly deaf be unable both to hear or to speak. Often, however, the effects of communication impairment may be less noticeable. Children, for example, who have a slight hearing loss due to 'glue ear', children with dyslexia or those with mild seizures all have their ability to communicate disrupted to some degree and this disruption may insidiously detract from their educational and general development.

Where there is more than one disability, communication problems and their resolution may be very complex. The communication problems facing deaf-blind children and those who wish to communicate with them are clearly enormous. The child who has a language disability and is also speech impaired may be denied the spoken practice of language structure which is vital if language skills are to develop. An alternative or augmentative means of communication will be necessary if language development is to proceed.

Many methods are available to help people who are disabled to communicate. Among these are writing aids, communication boards, E-Tran frames, hearing aids, sign and symbol systems, embossed text systems such as Braille and Moon, and page turners. In the past few years, the range of aids to communication has grown considerably. In particular, developments in microelectronics have made it possible greatly to enhance the learning opportunities for children with communication difficulties, particularly those who are physically disabled. Portable electronic communication aids, sometimes using synthesised speech, may assist communication face-to-face or over the telephone. Word processors can enable disabled people to write without handling paper while the computer can provide access to sources of information for those who cannot handle books in the normal way. In addition to providing children with physical and sensory handicaps access to the curriculum, the computer may also assist in modifying the curriculum for those who have moderate or severe learning difficulties.

In 1980, the government launched the Microelectronic Education Programme (MEP), a major initiative to promote the use of microelectronics in education. Some of the earliest applications of microcomputers in education were in the field of special education and, in particular, in schools for children with physical handicaps. Often drawing upon local technical knowledge, teachers in some of these schools helped develop new devices and computer programs to enable their children to communicate more effectively. The power and flexibility of these new systems, and their low cost compared with some of the electro-mechanical devices that had preceded them, made them increasingly attractive.

To promote and support the work with microelectronics in special education, MEP established four regional Special Education Microelectronics Resource Centres (SEMERCs). Initially, the SEMERCs were able to be quite closely involved with many of the new developments in communication aids and indeed to initiate some of them. However, as interest in the use of microcomputers began to develop among schools catering for other areas of special need, particularly the large number of schools for children with moderate learning difficulties, the SEMERC staff were not able to maintain the close involvement with individual children necessary to meet their communication needs. At the same time, a considerable amount of duplication and 're-invention' was occurring in many of the projects concerned with communication that were being initiated around the country.

In order to provide a national focus for the use of microelectronics in the field of communication aids in education, MEP established in May 1984 a new centre at Ormerod School, a special school for children with physical handicaps in Oxford. ACE stands for Aids to Communication in Education and the ACE Centre was given the task of gathering and disseminating information about microelectronic communication aids; developing a computer database of information about aids; liaising with manufacturers and others developing aids; providing an opportunity for people to see and try aids, devices and software for themselves, working with other centres concerned with communication; and supporting the work of the less specialist SEMERCs in the regions.

The school, its roll affected by changing patterns of disability and management, was able to provide the Centre with spacious self-contained accommodation. Within this area, there is a permanent display of equipment including portable computers and typewriters, switches, interfaces and special keyboards. The library area contains books, journals and other sources of information about communication in education, and information is also the focus of another area which houses the database and telecommunications equipment. An adjacent workshop enables devices to be constructed, modified and repaired when necessary. An office and other areas are used as workbases by members of staff and as workstations during in-service training workshops. For much of the time, however, the focus of the ACE Centre is the area set aside for working with children who visit with their parents, teachers, therapists and others in order that their communication needs may be assessed.

The staffing provided for the ACE Centre by MEP, and subsequently by its successor the Microelectronics Education Support Unit (MESU), comprised a Manager (later Director) and a Technical Consultant, both former teachers, and a Secretary. In addition to providing the accommodation and services, the host local authority seconded a teacher to the Centre for the first two years to act as Information Officer. The Nuffield Foundation granted funds to enable a half-time northern representative of the Centre to visit children in their schools and homes in the north of England from a base in Manchester. Over the first two years, the demands on the Centre developed rapidly. Hundreds of visitors, letters and telephone calls were received and many children were brought for assessment. The need for more staff rapidly became apparent. However, it became quickly clear also that, if children's communication needs were to be fully understood and properly assessed the skills of different professionals would need to be combined into a multi-disciplinary approach. Eventually, in 1986, a grant from the Gatsby Charitable Foundation made it possible to employ a speech therapist and an occupational therapist and so to establish this team. This grant made it possible to increase to full-time the northern representative and so to establish a satellite centre in Oldham.

In addition to answering the many telephone and written enquiries, a number of channels have been adopted for the task of dissemination. In such an innovative and rapidly developing field, those working in the field have little experience with which to compare the many items of software and hardware becoming available. In addition, such is the idiosyncratic nature of communication disabilities, experience with one child and one system may not be transferable to another. The Centre is therefore producing a range of evaluative surveys. The first three of these documents are 'Communication Aid Programs for the BBC Microcomputer'; 'Switches'; and 'Software' for use with children who have severe learning difficulties. The surveys are presented in loose-leaf form and are periodically updated.

These reference works have been well-received and many teachers and therapists have found them a valuable source of information and advice. However, as a medium for learning about the equipment and materials available, they are of course no substitute for 'hands-on' experience and face-to-face contact. To provide this contact, the ACE Centre staff have therefore been actively involved in in-service education and training. Workshops are organised in the Centre which are open to anyone concerned with children with communication difficulties. In addition to teachers and therapists, those attending these workshops have included parents, psychologists, advisers and education officers. The ACE Centre Workshops are held approximately monthly and such is the eagerness of those working in this field that they are often oversubscribed. Each workshop usually has a particular focus such as 'Severe Learning Difficulties', 'Portable Communication Aids' or 'Word Processors', although these titles do not preclude those attending from exploring other areas as time allows.

The Centre also holds monthly open afternoons which have a somewhat less structured format than the workshops. These provide opportunities to those interested perhaps to explore generally or to examine a particular combination of software and hardware, or to discuss a specific problem. Other Centre activities have included a three-day residential course which led to the development of a network of 'contact schools', day workshops for overseas visitors and an introductory day for education officers and advisers specifically concerned with special educational needs. In addition to these 'in-house' activities, ACE Centre staff have contributed to many courses and workshops held elsewhere around the country and abroad.

## ASSESSMENT OF COMMUNICATION NEEDS

Providing an opportunity for people to 'see and try aids for themselves' has developed into a major part of the ACE Centre's work. Children visit for assessment on three and sometimes four days every week. In the first four years, approximately 350 children were assessed and the waiting list for this service usually runs to 6 months. The development of a multi-professional assessment service was not specified in the Centre's brief; instead, this approach has been developed as a response to a need as perceived by the staff. Although at times, this interpretation of its brief has been an area of some debate, the response among those working in the field with communication impaired children would appear to leave no doubt that this perceived need is a felt need too.

Clearly, one small centre, however well equipped and staffed, could not be expected to provide a detailed assessment of all children with communication difficulties. Nor, indeed, should it attempt to do so. There are many children whose communication, and consequently learning opportunities, may be greatly enhanced through the use of an alternative approach, a readily available aid, a particular combination of hardware and software or a different method of management. With in-service education and training, the skills, knowledge and awareness necessary to meet these needs can be developed by teachers and therapists and applied locally in schools or centres. At this local level, children's needs can often be met more rapidly and more responsively. With the appropriate skills and knowledge, the teacher can then modify and adapt the methods selected as the child's needs change and develop.

Helping teachers and others to develop this awareness, through courses and workshops, will remain a vital part of the ACE Centre's work. However, while the needs of many children can be adequately met by school- or local authority-based assessment, there will remain a small number of children whose communication problems are so complex that the expertise necessary for their assessment will not be available and cannot be developed at local level.

Ideally, therefore, the Centre should only be seeing those children whose communication difficulties are so complex that they need specially adapted or innovative systems individually tailored to their needs. But many authorities are not yet able to provide guidance and advice even on existing devices. This means that the Centre is still asked by some authorities to see children whose problems are overcome with relative ease. An example might be a minimally brain-damaged child attending a mainstream school whose poor motor coordination is creating difficulties with written work. The child begins (often at secondary level) to fall behind because her or his work is untidy, brief and possibly tiring to achieve. Such children are unlike their peers, in that effort bears little relation to satisfying output. Frustration ensues and as the child becomes more discouraged, a downwards spiral is set in motion with poor self-image chasing decreasing effort.

The solution might well rest in the use of one of the portable electronic typewriters. These typewriters have many advantages over standard electric typewriters. They are fully portable and can therefore be carried from class to class and from school to home. They will run off rechargeable batteries, so that the user is not isolated from the rest of the class by needing to be near a wall socket. They are virtually silent and so do not disturb the concentration of others. They have memory facilities and also liquid crystal displays which give the children the chance to correct their work before it is committed to paper. These typewriters are available in High Street shops and are relatively cheap.

Although more authorities are becoming aware of the potential of such equipment for some children with special needs, many still seek advice from the Centre. Advice on readily available equipment of this kind should merely be a question of updating teachers, advisory teachers and advisers on the latest equipment through the Centre's workshops and surveys. Children are, however, still being sent (often over considerable distances) to the Centre for assessment for such equipment. This creates a long waiting list and the sheer numbers involved make it extremely difficult for satisfactory follow-up work to be carried out after the children have received their equipment.

One solution to this problem might be for the Centre, at this stage, to refuse to see all but the most complex cases. On the other hand it can be argued that the process of disseminating new ideas is inevitably slow and is best achieved by practical example. If one child makes good progress as the result of using some new equipment suggested by the Centre, teachers and others concerned will consider that equipment for other children in their authority. Some LEAs are developing resource centres and the most enlightened are seconding teachers specifically to the job of working in the special needs field with microtechnology. In some cases this is seen as giving teachers 'ACE time'. As so often in our educational system a solution to the problem is slowly evolving from the grass roots level.

For all assessments, complex or otherwise, the Centre has an 'open door' policy for referrals. Any one is free to refer a child and referrals come from parents as well as from a wide range of professionals including teachers, therapists, education officers, paediatricians, psychologists and social workers. The initial request for a visit is often made by telephone, during which time the child's difficulties are discussed and the expectations of the visit to the Centre considered prior to an appointment being made. It is important to ensure that equipment which might be suitable is available at the Centre for the child to try, and that there is not some nearer resource which might be tapped first. This second consideration is becoming increasingly important as the waiting list grows. If, after this initial discussion, it is decided that the child might benefit from a visit, a date is made and the LEA is informed. In this way, with the existing waiting list, the LEA has approximately six months in which to respond.

There is no charge for the children's visits and authorities are on the whole helpful in providing information which might be of assistance in the assessment. Information from the LEA may well include those parts of the child's statement which might be considered relevant to communication aid assessment. If so then the child is statemented. If not, there may be no LEA response, or the officer in charge of special needs may refer the Centre back to the child's school which will also have been approached. If the initial referral comes from the child's parents, they are asked to make sure that the school and any therapists involved are in agreement. Occasionally this causes difficulties. Some parents may feel that the school is not meeting the child's needs and they therefore seek outside support. Although it is fully recognised that parents and children are entitled to visit the Centre without involving the child's school or therapy team, such visits are rare as they are less likely to be beneficial. The equipment to be used must be accepted by all those working with the child. It is therefore most unusual for a child to attend the Centre without the full support of the school. In a few cases where this has happened, the children have been withdrawn from school by their parents, awaiting the outcome of an appeal against the provisions suggested in the statement.

Once general agreement has been reached by all concerned that a visit to the Centre might be beneficial to the child, background information forms are sent out to the parents and the school. The information received is used to prepare material appropriate to the child's physical ability and levels of cognitive and language function. Sometimes the information is scant and further telephone calls are necessary before a true profile of the child's functioning can be drawn up. On the other hand some schools will not only provide extensive and helpful reports from teachers and therapists but will also send photographs or even video tapes to illustrate switch difficulties.

Before the assessment, the Centre staff will meet together to discuss possible approaches. This initial discussion will include whomever is considered relevant to the forthcoming assessment. It could be that the child is non-speaking and severely physically impaired, in which case all the staff (technician, teacher, speech therapist and occupational therapist) will be involved. If, on the other hand, the child has no speech problem but needs a writing aid, the assessment might only involve a teacher and the occupational therapist. In the first example, the technician will be alerted to possible difficulties with existing switches and to the probable need for some immediate adaptations to be carried out. The other team members will consider the child's existing language function and prepare appropriate computer word lists or pictorial or symbol overlays for the Concept Keyboard.

Children come to the Centre to look specifically for microtechnological aids to their communication difficulties. However, such aids cannot be seen in isolation. 'Social communication' and 'communication for education' should not be two separate issues in the child's life with separate solutions to be separately funded by Health and Education. Many cerebral palsied individuals rely on the written word as their main communication channel. Portable devices such as the Canon Communicator, the QED memowriter or the Toby Churchill Lightwriter can be useful in some social situations but their effective use obviously depends on the development of reasonable literacy skills. With the positive language reinforcement and motivating experience of hearing synthesised speech, children using communication boards may increase their length of utterance from indicating only single key elements in a sentence to indicating two or three element phrases. A communication board can be made up of words, symbols, pictures or photographs to which the child points in order to 'talk'. Using the computer, speech synthesis and a programmable keyboard in this context is an educational exercise. The child is working on improving language structures, but the improvement in social communication abilities as a result will be obvious.

Non-electronic systems are therefore considered during the assessment alongside microelectronic aids. For example, the child using a communication board as described above may be able to use more areas of the board if it is colour-coded so that each area has several meanings depending on the colour chosen. Four colours, for example, could be placed at each corner of the board. Each area that the child can point to has four different messages or meanings. Each message is shaded in one of the four colours. The child indicates an area by pointing, fist pointing or eye pointing and then indicates one of the four corner colours, again by pointing or, if it is quicker, by eye pointing. In this way a child who previously had, say, twelve messages they could access, will have that number increased to forty-eight but each message will only take two movements.

Some of the children who come to the Centre have no reliable way of indicating 'yes' or 'no'. A simple solution to this problem might be to make coloured sweat bands with a 'yes' symbol embroidered on one and a 'no' symbol on the other. These are then worn on the wrists and the child can either look at the appropriate wrist or move it to indicate yes or no. Other children may be able to use a consistent sign for 'yes' and facial expression for 'no'. Such ideas are discussed with the child's parents and the school staff. Simple solutions still require planning and management in order for them to be successfully introduced and many visiting staff seem to welcome the opportunity to discuss their ideas with other professionals.

As technology improves with better quality speech production, with increased speed of processing, the better the potential for greater flexibility: smaller, more portable and compact units but with the possibility of different inputs; high-quality display panels for symbols or pictures, so the distinction between social and educational aids, between equipment for home and equipment for school, becomes less and less relevant. It is important therefore that the child's assessment at the ACE Centre considers the whole child and the interaction that takes place between the children and their environment, be it home or school. Such an assessment is only possible if the different disciplines work together as a team, not as independent professionals.

When the child arrives at the Centre everyone sits down together over a cup of coffee and a suggested plan for the day is discussed. There is much to learn during this discussion period. The staff will be watching exactly how and to whom the children are communicating. As nothing is being demanded of the child, at this stage, it can be a useful way of observing various behaviours important for the development of communication skills. Do the children initiate communication in any way? If they respond to spoken language, how simple or complex should that language be? Is the response better if spoken language is accompanied by signing (if the child is familiar with a particular system) or gesture? Do the children make eye contact with people with whom they are familiar and/or with people who are new to them? Do they indicate choice in some way? Do they respond to a question such as 'Do you want tea or coffee/ orange or lemon?' Or is the question automatically answered for them by parent or teacher? Physically, can the child hold a cup, hold a spoon, stir the coffee? The list is endless, but such initial observation is valuable and it is important that all the members of the team know what they are looking for. It is at this stage too that difficulties between home and school can be picked up. Sometimes simply by spending the day together, working with the child, such difficulties often stemming from different expectations can be ironed out or at least spoken about. Parents, teachers and therapists, seem to welcome the opportunity to get together for a whole day. Each may see the child in a new light.

The initial discussion period is also important as it gives the ACE staff and the visiting parents and professionals a little time to get to know each other before the child starts working with the equipment. The assessment is essentially achieved jointly by all those present. The ACE staff do not know the children. They do know the software, hardware and other equipment and they know from experience how it has helped other children. They also know the pitfalls. This knowledge must be matched to the child both as perceived in the Centre, on the particular day, and as she or he appears to parents, teachers and therapists at other times. It is interesting that the children will usually achieve more in the Centre than had been expected by those who accompanied them, rather than less, in spite of travelling long distances and being confronted by a strange situation and strange people. Indeed the comment has been made by one teacher, 'It's all very well for you in the Centre but he just won't do it like that back in the classroom'. The reason for the discrepancy is probably two-fold. In the first place, great care is taken to make a visit to the Centre fun. The approach is child-centred; it's different, a day out. Second, the Centre staff may well have high expectations of what the child can achieve and most children in this situation are anxious to live up to such expectations. Often too the children are experiencing real control for the first time. They become more important people in their own eyes. Care is also taken to ensure that the day is ended on a successful note and that the children take away some evidence of their hard work. This might be a printout of a picture drawn by hitting a switch just four times, a printout of their name or a letter to a member of the family not present. If the children are to use microtechnology daily to help them overcome their communication difficulties, the experience must be pleasurable and rewarding. None of us would choose to communicate with others if we felt we were being continually tested and under pressure to perform.

Once the child has started working, either on the computer or possibly with switches controlling a toy or tape recorder, a video system is set up, relayed to a different room so that some of the adults can see and hear what is happening without crowding around the child. This system also has the advantage of allowing a member of the ACE staff to explain what the child is doing and discuss the implications without disturbing the child's concentration. However it is equally important that the parents, teachers and therapists who will be working with the children in the future have the experience of working with them in the Centre as well. They therefore take it in turns to work with the child.

During the morning session it is hoped that the most appropriate switch and switch placement will have been chosen. Switches are not hand-held for the child to use as it is extremely difficult to ensure that the child is working independently if someone is holding the switch for them. Instead, once a position and switch have been chosen they are held in place by Orange Aids attached to the child's chair or table. When looking for the right switch it is important that the task being asked of the child is neither boring nor too complex. If it is boring the child may simply not see the point in trying. If, on the other hand, it is too complex, it will be difficult to work out why the child is not succeeding. It might not be the switch closure that is causing problems, but, for example, the fact that the child is being asked to understand a scanning system for the first time. Controlling a toy, a tape recorder, a little electric fan or other environmental device may initially be more appropriate than working the computer. Once a switch has been found or an appropriate keyboard selected, the child will begin to use software possibly with individual overlays for the Concept Keyboard or personalised wordlists.

During the lunch break the staff start to fill in a profile form on the child. This form is then used as a basis for the report writing. The lunch break can also be used to make different overlays, alter programs or adapt switches. More software and, if necessary, hardware is tried during the afternoon session. At the end of the afternoon there is a final discussion to ensure that everyone present is in agreement about the best equipment for the child. At this stage the problems of funding will be discussed and those of classroom management. If a computer is to be recommended, does the child need access to it on a daily basis or just a few times a week? If so, to what extent can the existing school equipment be used? Is a computer wanted as well for home? Should the child have his or her own computer at school which can be used at any time during the school day? If so, how will it be moved from room to room? Are there sufficient members of staff in the school able to ensure that the child receives maximum benefit from using the equipment? Who will work out a programme of work for the child? If the equipment is needed at home, who will show the parents how to use it so that they can work with their child? What about maintenance? What happens if the system breaks down? Does the local authority have a maintenance policy? Will it be happy to service this particular computer?

If a portable system is being recommended the same questions apply but the question of staff expertise may be even more crucial. If the portable device is a lap computer and therefore quite different from the computer in class, will the teacher concerned have the time or energy to master it before expecting the child to use it? Some portable communication systems such as Touch Talker are quite complex to set up for the user. Who will be responsible for this? The English company marketing Touch and Light Talker for Prenke Romich run workshops on the minspeak software used in the machines. Will a member of staff from school be released for a couple of days in order to attend such a workshop when it will benefit only one child in the school? Once again the list of questions is endless but they must be asked, as without satisfactory answers, the children will not benefit as they should from the potential offered by the new technology.

After the assessment the ACE staff again meet to discuss the report. This is then written by one of the therapists, further discussed with a teacher and finally sent to all those involved with the child, including the assistant education officer in charge of special needs in the child's local authority. At this point the ACE Centre's involvement officially ceases. Some children are being followed up more closely. Some ask for a further date to be made so that any problems can be ironed out and developments followed up with new suggestions. Others contact the Centre for specific advice about some of the recommendations. A quick phone call can be useful in this way. Such ad hoc arrangements, however, are not satisfactory, but until the waiting list is reduced there seems little that can be done to ensure a more satisfactory follow-up system.

In the future, when local provision is able to meet more of these children's needs, there will still remain some children whose difficulties are such that they need the combined expertise of experienced teachers, therapists and technicians to design systems which will enable them to communicate more effectively. It is this role that the ACE Centre should be fulfilling. There are too few children in need of such specialist help for it ever to be provided at a local level. Ideally there would be not one, but three closely coordinated centres working with local resources and involved not only with complex assessments and follow-up, but also with initial and in-service training for teachers, therapists and parents, as well as with the coordination of research and development to ensure that those who need it most get the full benefits of advancing technology.

# 14 SPECIAL NEEDS: THE COMMUNITY RESPONSE

Rhys Evans

## INTRODUCTION

The concept of special educational needs is invoked at the point at which circumstances are deemed to show that the mainstream provision of a school can no longer adequately provide for a given situation. Extra or alternative resources, human or material, are required to meet such needs. The concept as now defined in this country since 1981 is generous. It allows up to 20 per cent of a school population to present 'special needs', and requires these to be identified and met as appropriate. Resources are allowed accordingly. If a whole geographic area presents 'special needs', it can be designated a priority area, and again, after due diagnosis, special staffing and resources can be allowed. In cases of special need it is understood that no a priori solution exists. Thorough analysis, discussion and negotiation must be encouraged to lead to appropriate solutions.

Such solutions may require the breaking down of accepted barriers: the subject, the classroom, even the school. It may be that baby-care or dry-stone walling or dog breeding will provide part of the solution. The concept accepts this degree of flexible response and the system tries to provide the resources required.

Implicit in this analysis, however, is the notion that, however broadly and generously and flexibly it is defined, the management of special needs is a response to deviation from accepted norms planned for by the school and the curriculum. It is a form of crisis management.

## THE YOUTH SERVICE

It is relevant to contrast the structure of school education with what is in many authorities another branch of the education department: the youth service. Schooling is statutory and directly accountable through school governors to the LEA. Its curricula are usually divided into traditional specialisms which are teacher-led. Young people are organised into groups according to criteria decided upon by the staff. Discipline is reinforced with a system of sanctions and controls. Increasing political control of public education ensures that it responds to the economic needs of the country.

Youth work is a far more nebulous concept. It hovers between the statutory and voluntary sectors. Different authorities manage it under different departments. Its workers have a variety of different titles, and the titles change periodically. There is continuous argument about what it is and what it is for. There is no rational agreement in training courses for youth workers and consequently there is enormous variety, even within the statutory system.

Nevertheless it has certain clear characteristics. It does not base its activity on particular specialisms. It aims to meet the needs of the young people it works with. It works through negotiation and organises with the participation of its client group. Its curriculum is social education including provision for leisure and recreation. It works with young people in their own social-peer groupings rather than in groupings decided upon by the staff. As far as the client group is concerned, attendance is voluntary.

Increasingly, and particularly in community schools, school and youth service work closely together and, since their structure and methods are directly contrary, there can be a valuable complementarity between them. In such cases, school is the orthodox mainstream and youth service joins in the provision for special needs. Even so, the model of 'standard' and 'deviation' is unchanged, and youth service is forced into the role of crisis management.

The crisis management model is by far the commonest. Its message is simple. Standardise as far as you reasonably can and make appropriate provision for deviation. Philosophically it is safe, in that it maintains a conservative orthodoxy as far as possible. Economically it is sound in that it is cheaper than more radical models.

But radical models do exist. They are to be found in a number of countries, especially in the Third World, where socialist projects are being undertaken, or in areas of Europe where, often, it appears that all else has failed. It is no coincidence that they are often inspired by the writings and practice of Paulo Freire, whom I shall invoke extensively in this chapter. And what they have in common with each other is the element of negotiated learning, self-generated learning, community-based learning: in other words direct involvement with the planning and execution of the learning process.

I shall look briefly at three examples of educational situations with special reference to the element of negotiated learning, the local community arena in which they occur, and the part it plays in the learning process.

## THE KIEZSCHULE

Kreuzberg is a quarter of West Berlin with a large Turkish population. Children growing up in this area experience learning difficulties associated with social and economic factors external to themselves. They are part of an immigrant population in an inner city area. Many adults and school leavers are unemployed, and, as an ethnic group they are marginalised. There are considerable cultural obstacles to their integration with the indigenous community. One of the major manifestations of this is language.

It can be argued that children growing up in a bilingual situation have an educational and cultural advantage. Many young people in Wales have the benefit of two languages, two cultures, two inheritances which have been well integrated and which by now have become accepted as of equal value. In the context of recent immigration, however, the bilingual split divides the language of home from the transactional language of the outside world and, for children, of school. We see this most clearly in England in the Bangladeshi populations and in the clash between West Indian English as spoken in the home and the street and standard English as required in the classroom.

In 1985 a new school opened in Kreuzberg which from the start attempted to initiate a radical programme in response to local needs. An attractively produced brochure of 'Information for Parents' was published in Turkish and German proclaiming in simple language the aims of the Kiezschule, or neighbourhood school, Kiez being a local colloquialism for a sector of the city.

> We the teachers in the Kiezschule know from experience that many students come to us with a sense of disappointment and resignation. These young people often find school boring and no longer want to come. No more patience with Maths and German. But the same students, faced with just as difficult problems out of school, show patience and skill, when for example they are making and mending, building or bodging or making music. That's why we are starting a school where students can develop these very skills and in this way learn the things they need in their lives and their jobs. And working in the Kiezschule, students and parents and teachers together, will be fun.

The main strategies of the school in its attempt to provide an appropriate learning environment are continuity and coherence, provided by organising students into small groups with permanent teams of Turkish and German teachers; consciousness of the language difficulties and an attempt to provide a bilingual learning and social environment; and above all - reflecting the title of the school - an emphasis on learning within the community. The latter contains social and psychological counselling, legal advice, cultural activity, do-it-yourself, and need not happen within the school buildings. The resources of the community are exploited both inside and outside the school itself.

The school day begins with breakfast. The staff consider this most important, especially after the week-end, to tease away the language barriers between school and home. Over tea, bread and olives, a linguistic limbering up takes place. When classes start, the team situation always ensures that Turkish and German speaking adults are in the classroom to help create the learning environment.

> The name "Kiezschule" indicates that for our students learning in the community and about the community

> is and always will be a self-evident part of what they do.
>
> This means that community-based learning will always emphasize the connections between learning and living, education and real life, school and community.
>
> The most important question is always: Where can I get assistance or advice? Where are things getting done? Or what can I myself do to change my own existence?

The conviction that lies behind this school experiment, desperately needed in that part of Berlin where disaffection and despair predominate, is that people do learn and do want to learn and that learning is a basic human need. The task of the school is to complement and support the learning which is already taking place, to understand the directions in which people want to or need to go, and to be an agent for political change in so far as it acts, for the students, as a bridge between their inner and outer worlds. The community therefore, is a vital ingredient in the curriculum of such a school, or expressed in a negative way, without involvement in the community the radical convictions of such a school could not be translated into practice, would fossilise or die.

The disadvantage of the Kiezschule experiment is that it is the only one of its kind and thus only caters for around 300 pupils. Its advantage is that it shows what can be achieved when a large amount of public money is put into a scheme, not only for appropriate buildings but also for staff. The school's human resources were enhanced at the start by 11.5 extra social work, youth work and community work staff. In Germany these workers are called Sozialpadagogen and are trained differently from community workers in Britain. In many other schools, trying to tackle similar problems in similar environments, the benefits of new buildings, extra staff and time for careful planning has not been available. All too often the management of special needs amounts to little more than the daily management of crisis. Nevertheless, the ways in which the challenge is met, in different countries and different circumstances, show remarkable similarities. In a school a young person, or group, will show boredom, or unwillingness to participate, or disaffection, and this leads through a number of conflicts or confrontations to crisis.

At the moment of crisis all parties are forced to acknowledge that the mainstream curriculum, or parts of it, have been inappropriate, and forced to look for 'alternatives' which will prove more appropriate. The school and the disaffected pupils are forced to negotiate. Negotiation becomes a last-ditch activity and the setting up of 'alternatives' a last-ditch solution.

The implication here is the idea that a negotiated learning process is only appropriate or necessary, or economically feasible, for a few special people in times of crisis, and what is set up as a result is an 'alternative', sometimes called an 'alternative curriculum', implicitly less desirable and often more expensive than the mainstream system up for everywoman and everyman in the summer term preceding the year of its operation. Special needs have the characteristics of being unorthodox, expensive, and administratively inconvenient. But a radical school, in the sense that it goes to the roots of a question, will have no 'alternatives' for they will be its mainstream, and will make an orthodoxy out of negotiation, rather than reserving it as a crisis-management technique.

Freire (1972) defines what he has called a 'banking education' which assumes that students are a kind of bank account into which currency is inserted. They are 'receptacles to be filled by the teacher' and 'knowledge is a gift bestowed by those who consider themselves knowledgeable upon those whom they consider to know nothing'. This form of education reinforces existing social and political structures. It encourages acceptance and discourages original thought. With it is contrasted what he calls 'problem-posing education': 'The banking method emphasizes permanence and becomes reactionary. Problem-posing education, which accepts neither a well-behaved pre-set nor a pre-determined future, roots itself in the dynamic present and becomes revolutionary.'

Here Freire's argument affects us directly. He says that the 'point of departure must always be the "here-and-now" which constitutes the situation within which they are submerged, from which they emerge, and in which they intervene'. Revolutionary education can only derive from people's immediate circumstances, from their understanding and interpretation of the 'here-and-now'. In these terms, education which is separated from the social, political and economic fabric in which people exist can only be a form of 'banking education'.

The relevance of this observation to the argument of this chapter is that again and again the management of special needs, whether considered as a last-ditch alternative, as special treatment for an otherwise unmanageable minority, or as a new, radical mainstream, involves negotiation, and a basis in the processes of the real environment, the community. Wherever a school may stand within this spectrum, whether it totally rejects negotiation and community-based learning, or whether it seeks to create a new radical mainstream as described, its role is inescapably political: one way or the other, by acceptance or rejection, it responds to the community and the community responds to it.

## THE COMMUNITY COMPREHENSIVE SCHOOL

In the University Community Comprehensive School in Liverpool, the local communities permeate the institution in a number of ways. The school was an amalgamation of three existing schools. The arbitrary thrusting together of several different communities in this way has generated innumerable tensions. Racial conflict and the increasing social fragmentation of the area are reflected in the school, and the dramas play themselves out in classroom and corridor.

The political undercurrents of any community move fast, but nowhere more than in areas of high unemployment and racial tension. Popular attitudes to the institutions of society change, and in no time schools come to be seen as a symbol of a repressive establishment. But schools are still a more finely-tuned reflector of social processes than perhaps any other institution, and every nuance of a community can be found played back in the arena of the school.

In contrast to the Kiezschule, the Community Comprehensive School's response to its community has been a management of crisis from the moment it opened, and this has been immeasurably taxing on its staff. The community permeates the school in another sense. In responding to crisis and setting up alternatives it has welcomed into the school a variety of people and organisations who are collaborating with the professional staff. There are also on the staff some who have lived and worked in the community for as long as thirty years and have grown up with its people and its problems.

A group known as 'The Diggers', for instance, started off eleven years ago as a Job Creation Scheme, then became a STEP scheme and now operates under the Community Programme. In all they have some 120 employees, and are chiefly involved with developing public gardens, including gardens for the disabled. They have acquired a base in the school and work with many young people on gardening projects, a travelling farm, a new city farm, painting murals around the school - a variety of activity almost without boundaries. One could not overlook the presence of The Diggers and their work with young people in that school. Yet their involvement was not part of an overall plan. It was one of the things which happened in response to need.

The Community Service Volunteers also have a base in the school and a permanent worker on site. They work with young people in close cooperation with the school staff, believing that 'a relevant education for children of all abilities should relate closely to the real world and to the real community in which children live'. It is clear that their efforts have involved and excited a number of young people not only in 'well established communities where opportunities for learning were great, but also where unemployment was high and where the future for young people was bleak'.

Two members of the special needs team themselves used to run an open-house project for young and old in the neighbourhood, which is obviously still a cherished memory of effective local work and forms part of their own deep roots in the community. Since it opened, the school has met the challenges which occurred, accepting help wherever it was offerred, basing its response to crisis, wherever possible, on the resources of the community which generated the need. One example of this process was the 'Christmas Extravaganza 1986'.

In December of that year the Liverpool Star celebrated with a photograph and an article an event called 'Extravaganza' organised by a group of fifth-year students at the Community Comprehensive School, and hiding behind the photograph was a story of months of effort and negotiation to involve a group of disaffected young people in personal investment in a project which had meant something to them. Six months previously a four-page document had been circulated internally in the school, highlighting the need for an alternative curriculum for this self-same group, for the abandonment of their present timetable, for generous staffing, a modular/topic/project approach to learning, practical rather than academic methods of learning and understanding, a negotiated timetable, deschooling for approximately half the week...the result, six months later, was 'Extravaganza'.

The 1986 document quoted above was an appeal to staff to respond to what was being identified as a crisis. The structure of the situation was what I have described as a crisis-management structure. In other words, there is an orthodoxy which, other things being equal, everyone accepts. In times of crisis, the orthodoxy becomes flexible and people respond accordingly until such time as a new kind of balance is achieved. I have argued that, in much of Europe at any rate, this is the model of response most commonly found, and its fundamental assumption, however flexible its response to crisis may be, is that the orthodox curriculum is by and large sound.

The 'radical' model does not make this assumption. Indeed, it makes a contrary assumption. It assumes that 'banking education' creates ignorance by stifling thought and producing either resigned silence or active disaffection.

We have to accept that the education system in Britain is anything but radical. There is pressure from the political right and the political left, each for different reasons, to determine the curriculum externally. The right is moving resolutely towards centralisation and criterion-referenced testing so that the economic investment in education should better serve the wealth of the country. The left hotly defends the comprehensive school, mixed ability learning and the core curriculum, in defence of its political concept of equal right and equality of opportunity. Neither, for their own reasons, will tackle student participation or community involvement in the stuff of education, the content and structure of the curriculum, any more than will the teachers' unions. Almost the only areas in which, as we have seen, 'negotiation' and 'alternatives' are envisaged are those last-ditch situations where all else has falled: that is, special needs.

But there is another area, on the periphery of school, in which the 'special needs' approach is accepted and time-hallowed. This is what was once called the Youth Service and is now often referred to as Community Education (Youth). We saw that in the Kiezschule some 11.5 Sozialpadagogen were appointed when the school first opened, as a supplement to the school staff. Here and there in this country, too, where the need has been seen to be great, and special, similar appointments have been made. Though, they have rarely violated the sanctity of the mainstream curriculum, they have often been used to avert crisis and introduce a degree of negotiation into the way in which schools fortunate enough to have them are run.

## GROBY COMMUNITY COLLEGE

One of the significant characteristics of so-called Phase 3 community colleges in Leicestershire is the fact that the Head of Community Education is a full vice-principal with a status in the hierarchy equal to the conventional vice-principals or deputy heads. This meant, at Groby Community College, one of the first Phase 3 colleges, which opened in 1977, that planning for the community involvement of all staff proceeded at the same level as all other aspects of the school's programme. Another significant characteristic was the fact that all staff had the right to opt for part of their teaching time to be given to community education. Consequently, a good number were closely involved with the community from the start.

Some of the college's best experience was gained during a period when it became heavily involved with the rebuilding and refurbishment of the old primary school in the village, and its conversion into Groby Village Hall. It was a period of some eighteen months when the local community, together with local unemployed young people, an MSC-funded Community Enterprise Programme, and large numbers of young people still at school worked together 'without frontiers' on a large project on behalf of the community. During that period there was a real coherence between different parts of the community, between ages and classes. Mutual respect was derived from collaboration on the project. The school operated on two bases, and a flow of students moved backwards and forwards between the two. It was a place of work and of recreation. All kinds of special needs were met. There were no experts and a thousand problems to be solved. One of the most interesting by-products of the project was the development of people's skill with language, not only the language of analysis and problem-solving, but also the language of sights and sounds and emotions and relationships.

In subsequent years, long after the Village Hall project had come to an end, and with it much of the valuable coherence which had been engendered, the college continued to pursue the arguments and debates which had come to life during that time, couched in the notion of 'appropriate curriculum' and the constant tension between 'orthodox' and 'unorthodox' curriculum. The college was well aware that its own structure was not 'radical', and that its management of special needs followed the 'crisis management' model. Nevertheless, it was feeling its way towards a compromise.

Between 1984 and 1985 a series of discussion papers on Appropriate Curriculum were written and became the basis of action. The first defined the terms. The characteristics of 'appropriate curriculum' are that:

- it is adapted to real learning needs;
- it is adapted to an individual's or group's own learning processes;
- it is developmental and its products are incidental to the process;
- it is adapted to a particular physical, social and cultural environment;
- it maximises the use of the resources of its physical, social and cultural environment.

(Appropriate Curriculum, April, 1984)

In other words, 'appropriate curriculum' springs from the needs of the students and the community, and is not designed, from the outside, to serve the demands of the country's economy, to generate the country's wealth.

The consensus of staff agreed that in order to support the 'appropriate curriculum' a reorientation of the arithmetic of the pupil-teacher ratio was necessary. The Curriculum Support Team (CST) is by now quite a large inter-faculty group, all of whom have part of their teaching time kept free, so that it can be applied to working, in or out of class, with individuals or groups on negotiated activity. All staff pay the price of this reorientation, either in terms of slightly higher class numbers or slightly fewer non-teaching periods. The baseline of the account remains the same.

The last discussion paper, written almost a year later, examines the tension between the orthodox and the unorthodox curriculum.

> Our curriculum is our institutional orthodoxy. It is 'where we stand' at present, taking into consideration all the current constraints of staffing, training, resourcing and finance.
>
> While we accept and honour our standing orders, however, and protect our formal network, we at the same time criticise them, we often find them inadequate to perform the role of providing an education appropriate to all our students.
>
> Having designed, constructed and subscribed to the orthodox curriculum, many of us regularly behave in an unorthodox manner within it. Indeed, most of us, I suggest, have an orthodox and an unorthodox side to our nature: one respecting the security of a stable system, the other often actively rebelling against it.
>
> Groby Community College has trodden an unusual path in this respect. It has always had its orthodox curriculum, but from its earliest days there has been a strong element of unorthodoxy, even among its hierarchical leaders, which has challenged and even subverted its institutional stability.
>
> It has recently gone further than this. The unorthodox curriculum is not merely tolerated as an element of flexibility: it operates side by side with the formal network with equal sanctity and equal encouragement. The orthodox and the unorthodox are designed to support each other.
>
> (Appropriate Curriculum, January, 1985)

Maybe this can be described as a compromise position, a model still unambiguously forged in the orthodox mould, but recognising, legitimising and timetabling for the unorthodox, not to say subversive activity. It is a boat in which teachers, youth workers, parents, old-age pensioners, parish councillors, and a host of other people of all ages row together. It is a boat designed to tolerate a degree of rocking.

Every member of a school or college has special educational needs, and every member of a school or college does learn and does want to learn. Only, as the brochure of the Kiezschule suggested, much of this learning takes place outside school. Important questions for community education are therefore: how and what do our students learn, and what role is there for trained, professional educators in this process? A danger within orthodox, a priori curricula is that they do not ask questions, and indeed, implicitly, give diminished status to areas in which extra-curricular learning takes place: the supermarket, the bathroom, the garage, the garden, the funeral, the wedding, the moment of love or betrayal. For example, at the moment of writing, I know that young people in my community are talking about AIDS and questioning seriously the conventional gender roles of young men and young women within their existing youth culture. I know, too, that young women find this issue easier to discuss and to tackle than young men. What structures exist to help young men today to cope with what may be a dramatic change in their role from now on? Can 'special needs' do justice to a challenge of this kind?

## REFERENCE

Freire, P. (1972) Pedagogy of the Oppressed, Harmondsworth: Penguin.

# INDEX

# Index